Charging for Computer Services: Principles and Guidelines

This book was written under the
auspices of the Planning Council
on Computing in Higher Education
and Research. The Planning Council
is an activity within EDUCOM,
a consortium of universities and
colleges dedicated to improving
the use of information technology
in higher education.

Dan Bernard
EDUCOM

James C. Emery
EDUCOM

Richard L. Nolan
D. P. Management Corporation

Robert H. Scott
Harvard University

Charging for Computer Services: Principles and Guidelines

PBI
a petrocelli
book
new york / princeton

Library of Congress Cataloging in Publication Data
Main entry under title:

Charging for computer services.

  Bibliography: p.
  Includes index.
  1. Data processing service centers—Fees.
I. Bernard, Dan.
HF5548.2.C475   658.8'16   77-23811
ISBN 0-89433-055-1
ISBN 0-89433-051-9 pbk.

CONTENTS

PREFACE

Charging internally for the use of central computer facilities is now a common organizational practice. A charge-out policy can play a major role in promoting effective and efficient utilization of computing resources. In practice, however, charging all too often fails to have a significant beneficial impact, and indeed can be a major source of tensions and user dissatisfaction. Charge-out systems are most likely to be successful when they are based on an understanding of the purposes underlying charging and the requirements for it to be effective. This monograph is intended to contribute to such an understanding.

A central element in our approach is the view that charge-out should be regarded not simply as a cost allocation mechanism, but as a tool for management control. Like all management control devices, a charge-out system needs to be tailored to the objectives it is to serve and the circumstances within which it will operate. Therefore, the monograph does not attempt to specify a single "correct" or "ideal" form of charge-out system; instead, we lay out design principles, considerations, and alternatives so as to provide guidance in dealing with any particular situation. The terms of the discussion have been deliberately kept general, and it should therefore be applicable to any type of organization.

One of the difficulties that arises with charge-out is that it is an area in which there are few clear-cut answers. Charging can be approached in many ways, and there is considerable lack of agreement as to the nature of the problems, let alone the solutions! This monograph, therefore, inevitably reflects the authors' own viewpoints. Readers may well disagree with some of our conclusions. Nevertheless, if in the process we provoke thought on issues that might otherwise have remained unexamined, we will have accomplished our main purpose.

Several people reviewed the draft; particular thanks are due to Norman Nielsen, Carl Palmer, David Solomons, and Al Jones. Thanks are also due to Dot Belza, Phoebe Wechsler, and Jane Wheatley for their skill in typing the drafts and the final manuscript. Responsibility for the contents, of course, rests entirely with the authors.

D.B., J.C.E., R.L.N., R.H.S.
May 1977

1 / INTRODUCTION

Management control has been defined as "the process by which managers assure that resources are obtained and used effectively and efficiently in the accomplishment of the organization's goals."[1] Assuring effectiveness and efficiency in the provision and use of computing resources is one aspect of the management control problem. Moreover, several factors have made it an increasingly important aspect:

Computing now plays a critical role in most organizations of significant size. In many cases most of the key organizational functions are dependent on computer-based systems and services.

Expenditure on computing has grown with the range and scale of applications and now represents a significant proportion of most organizational budgets. A 1968 survey of industrial firms found

[1]R. N. Anthony, J. Dearden and R. F. Vancil, *Management Control Systems* (Homewood, Ill.: R. D. Irwin, 1972).

that computer-related expenditures averaged around one percent of sales;[2] a more recent sample provided a similar average, with individual cases ranging up to four percent.[3] Data published for a group of universities in 1971 showed an even higher level of expenditure on computing in this sector—over two percent of total budget on average.[4]

As Martin Robbins has noted,[5] a form of Parkinson's Law operates in relation to computing—work load tends to fill available capacity. Experience has shown that without some effective means of control, computer resources have a particularly strong tendency to be used ineffectively and inefficiently, while demand for computing seems capable of growing without apparent limit.

Studies of the pattern of development of computing within organizations have shown that charge-out systems are typically introduced by management in response to a perceived need to improve control over computing activities.[6] The main objective behind this decision is normally to bring computing within the

[2] *Unlocking the Computer's Profit Potential* (McKinsey & Co., 1968).
[3] R. L. Nolan, *Management Accounting and Control of Data Processing* (National Association of Accountants, June 1977).
[4] *The Financing and Organization of Computing in Higher Education: 1971* EDUCOM, 1971, p. 8.
[5] M. D. Robbins, W. S. Dorn and J. E. Skelton, *Who Runs the Computer?* (Boulder: Westview Press, 1975), p. 63.
[6] R. L. Nolan, "Managing the Computer Resource: A Stage Hypothesis," *Communications of the ACM,* vol. 16, no. 7, (July 1973), pp. 399–405, and C. F. Gibson and R. L. Nolan, "Managing the Four Stages of EDP Growth," *Harvard Business Review,* vol. 52, no. 1, (January-February 1974).

framework of responsibility accounting, which forms the basis for management control in most organizations. Charging has by no means solved all the problems of controlling computer activities and, indeed, has sometimes given rise to some new ones. Nevertheless, it has proved to be an important management tool. The use of charging has grown steadily, and is now normal practice: in a 1975 survey by the Cost Accounting Standards Board, over seventy percent of the organizations polled operated some form of charge-out scheme.[7] Moreover, Nolan's "Stages of Growth" studies[8] indicate that, as organizations become more mature in their use of computers, charge-out systems play an increasingly significant role. Thus, their importance seems likely to continue to grow.

A charge-out system, like any management control tool, must be designed in relation to the particular situation involved. The features best suited to a particular organization will depend on the nature of its computing activities, the sophistication of its users, and other factors unique to that organization. For example, an installation providing on-demand batch processing or time-sharing services on a "job-shop" basis requires different charging arrangements than one that carries out routine administrative data processing.

More significantly, the design of a charge-out system must reflect management's objectives in controlling computing activities and the role that manage-

[7]D. H. Li, *Accounting for Costs of EDP Service Centers* (Cost Accounting Standards Board, 441 G St., Wash., D.C. 20548, 1975).
[8]Nolan, op. cit.

ment wishes charging to play in the control process. The importance of the role assigned to a charge-out system can vary considerably, ranging from simple "funny-money" schemes that act as little more than resource rationing devices, to financially oriented systems that play a central role in the organization's decisions on computing expenditure and allocation.

In view of this, the next chapter begins by examining the objectives that potentially may be pursued through charging. This discussion establishes the background for the remainder of the book, in which the primary concern is to show how the characteristics of a charge-out system can be designed to suit any particular set of objectives and circumstances.

2 / OBJECTIVES IN CHARGING

Management's objectives in charging for computer services may vary from one organization to another. Nevertheless, the primary objectives are typically all related in some way to *control* of the organization's computing activities. In this chapter we consider the broad aims normally associated with management control of computing, and the functions that charging can fulfill in relation to these aims. In addition, we discuss some of the dangers that are inherent in viewing charging purely as a cost allocation mechanism without considering the objectives underlying this allocation process.

The Management Control Problem

Management needs to be concerned with several aspects of an organization's computing activities. At the operational level, it must try to ensure that users em-

5

ploy the computing resources available to them effectively and efficiently.[1] At the same time, the computer center itself must be encouraged to operate efficiently and to be responsive to users' needs. Finally, in a job-shop environment where users have free access to computing resources, there is a need to limit total demand for these resources to the available capacity and to minimize the problems caused by congestion and variations in load.

Over and above these operational concerns, management is also faced with fundamental resource allocation decisions related to computing. Specifically, it must:

Achieve an appropriate balance between expenditure on computing and expenditure in other areas.

Allocate computing expenditure to the most cost-effective combination of computing resources—particularly in balancing expenditures among central facilities, distributed systems, and outside services.

Deploy the available computing resources among users and application areas in a way that yields maximum benefit for the organization as a whole.

---

[1]Our distinction between effectiveness and efficiency is essentially that between "doing the right things" and "doing things right." In this context, *effectiveness* is a function of the choice of applications for computer resources, while *efficiency* is concerned with the cost of the resources used in the applications. Clearly, both are involved in obtaining maximum benefit from computing expenditure.

Associated with these concerns is a problem that arises specifically from the shared nature of most computing resources. For a combination of technical and economic reasons, computer hardware and system development, or both, are normally centralized—or at least partially centralized, so that most internal computer services are provided by shared facilities supporting several user departments within an organization or major organizational unit. But, unlike most central support functions, computing typically has major significance in terms of its cost, complexity, and importance as a key resource. Moreover, there are potentially great variations in both cost and quality of computer services. These factors tend to generate strong pressures from user departments to gain direct control of their computing activities on the same basis as other major resources such as personnel, supplies, etc. The same factors also tend to make such decentralization of control desirable. The problem that arises, therefore, is to decentralize control effectively when the resources involved are shared between the user departments, and when many of the key issues relating to computing can only be properly decided from an organizationwide perspective.

Functions of a Charge-Out System

Consider now the functions of charging in relation to these tasks. All charge-out systems consist of two interdependent components:

A *budgeting process* through which the organization plans the provision of computing resources and determines their internal allocation.

A *pricing scheme* that measures, and provides a basis for controlling, users' consumption of these resources.

The combination can support the management control objectives discussed above in several ways. In particular, it can:

Provide cost information for management control and decision making

Provide a means of rationing resources among competing users

Encourage users to employ computing resources effectively and efficiently

Promote effective and efficient provision of services by the computer facility

Permit decentralization of control over the resource allocation decisions associated with computing

These functions are discussed further below. We should first point out, however, that in each case we are discussing functions that charging *can* perform. The functions actually performed by any particular charge-out system will depend on management's view of the role charging should play in the overall management control process associated with computing, and on the extent to which the charge-out system has been designed to carry out effectively its intended functions.

Provision of Cost Information. The pricing scheme provides information on the resource costs associated with current and proposed applications, alternative technical strategies, etc., and thus can provide guidance for management decisions on computing activities. Also, to the extent that computing charges are properly integrated into the organization's management accounting system, charging can ensure that computing costs are taken into account in evaluating the performance of individual organizational units and in making general organizational decisions such as product pricing.

Rationing of Resources. In a routine administrative processing environment the allocation of computer center resources within the organization is essentially determined through the choice of application systems implemented. However, where users can directly control their usage of resources—as, for example, in an installation providing general-purpose "job-shop" batch and time-sharing services—some means is required of rationing the available resources among the competing users. Without an explicit rationing mechanism, the allocation is established by default through competition for the facility's services; as Nielsen has pointed out, "if resource allocation is not done explicitly, it will be done implicitly; there is no such thing as 'no allocation.' "[2] It is obviously unlikely that the latter approach will produce the most desirable distribution of resource usage.

By providing a mechanism for planning and controlling computer usage, a charge-out system allows the distribution of resources to be determined explicitly through an explicit, and presumably rational, budgeting process. This rationing action of charge-out not only helps ensure that computing resources are distributed in a way that consciously balances the needs of different user areas, but also provides each user area with a clear indication of the resources it will have available.

Apart from this overall allocation problem, a computer facility also needs to allocate, on a day-to-day basis, priority for access to resources under congested conditions; this problem again tends to be most significant in a job-shop environment. Charging can also play a role with respect to this short-term allocation problem. By setting up a charging structure in which prices vary with service level demanded or time of day, the organization can essentially set up an internal market for access priority in which users can be left to determine their priority themselves based on the price they are prepared to pay for it.

Promoting Effective and Efficient Use of Resources. With charging, the user sees computing as a commodity with a cost, rather than a free good. Given effective

[2]Norman R. Nielsen, "The Allocation of Computer Resources—Is Pricing the Answer?" *Communications of the ACM,* vol. 13, no. 8 (August 1970), pp. 467–474.

budgetary control, charging also limits the availability of computing to users, turning it into a scarce resource from their point of view. These factors tend to produce a major beneficial change in user attitudes and behavior toward their use of computing. Moreover, the charging structure also communicates to users the cost of the resources involved, and can therefore guide them in making cost-effective use of these resources.

Charging can influence user behavior at several levels. First, it discourages waste of resources. An excellent illustration of this is provided by an incident described by Nielsen:

> . . . an acute shortage of magnetic tapes had developed at the Campus Facility of the Stanford Computation Center. Users were reserving tapes at an ever increasing rate; yet they were releasing very few tapes. Pleas were made for users to release all tapes that were not absolutely essential for their work, but this met with almost no response. Finally, in an attempt to cover the mounting tape costs, management decided to levy a nominal charge of $1/tape/month. On the first day that the charge was instituted more than 1/3 of the "absolutely essential" reserved tapes were released. Management has been a firm believer in pricing ever since.[3]

Second, charging encourages users to make cost-effective use of resources in their computing applications. For example, a research user might be led to design his programs efficiently so as to minimize his charges. In another case, a manager might eliminate a regularly printed report whose value did not justify the

[3]Norman R. Nielsen, "Flexible Pricing: An Approach to the Allocation of Computer Resources," *Proceedings AFIPS Fall Joint Computer Conference, 1968.*

cost of producing it. As yet another example, comparison of the relative charges involved might lead a user to make a cost-effective choice between on-line and batch operation for a new application.

At the highest level, a charge-out system can assist in effective deployment of computer resource among applications by encouraging users to select the most cost-effective uses for their computing funds.

It is important to recognize, however, that the fact that users are charged for computing is not sufficient in itself to ensure that charging will have the effects discussed above. The pricing scheme for computer resources must be economically sound, so that user efforts to reduce their charges do in fact result in improved efficiency. More significantly, if the user is to be expected to control and intelligently seek ways of reducing his charges, he must be provided with the information necessary to do so; in particular, he must understand the basis on which the charges are made. Finally, the budgetary framework must exert genuine pressure on the user; computer charges need to be explicitly focused on within the management control process, and control exerted not only at the level of budget administrators, but also down through the organization to the end users, whose behavior primarily determines the way computing resources are used. Failure to recognize these prerequisites is probably the main cause of ineffective charge-out policies.

Promoting Cost-Effective Provision of Computer Services. By providing information on the cost of centrally provided computer services, charging can assist in the cost-effective deployment of funds among the central facility, distributed resources and outside services.

Charging also can promote efficiency, together with quality of service, at the computer center itself. First, it provides management information that can assist in control of the center's operations. Second, by placing users in the position of customers who are paying for service, it generates market pressures that can promote efficiency and responsiveness to local needs. Third, the center can use the pricing scheme to influence the pattern of demand, so as to achieve balanced utilization of resources; an example of this is the use of discounts for overnight processing to smooth installation loading.

Decentralization of Control over Computing. Charge-out can be used primarily as an operational control tool, while the basic policy decisions on the scale of computing expenditures and their deployment are controlled centrally. In this case, the functions of charging are largely limited to those discussed above. However, charging can also be used as a means of decentralizing these policy-level resource allocation decisions within the organization.

Users can be given a total budget for computing and left to make their own decisions as to how these funds will be deployed among alternative uses, based on their judgment of the relative value of these alternatives. Furthermore, users can be given control over the size of their computing budgets. By integrating the computer charge-out system with the organization's financial budgeting and control mechanisms and treating computer charges on the same basis as "real" cash expenditures, each budgetary unit can be left to choose the proportion of its total budget to be spent on computing, based on its own perception of the tradeoff between this and other uses of funds. Thus, rather than the organization determining centrally the size of the total computing budget and its internal allocation, these decisions can be made implicitly through a combination of individual choices.

Finally, charging can also be used to give users more freedom to choose *where* they spend their computing funds—at the central facility, on their own minicomputer, or on outside services—thereby decentralizing decisions on the distribution of expenditures between these alternatives.

Decentralization along these lines can provide major benefits. It brings computing within the framework of the organization's overall management control system, providing users with control over their own computing activities, and reducing the need for special central administrative mechanisms dealing specifically with computing. These central mechanisms, which are often overloaded, distorted by political pressures, and unresponsive to changing conditions, are replaced with impersonal, economically oriented market mechanisms. Moreover, expanding of the role of charging in this way greatly strengthens its action in influencing user attitudes and behavior and in promoting efficient and responsive performance on the part of the computer facility.

The key question, of course, is the extent to which users' choices in a decentralized environment will be consistent with the organization's overall interests and objectives. This issue, and others associated with decentralization of control, are discussed at a later stage. Ultimately, though, management must make its own judgment as to the extent to which it is prepared to decentralize control to users, based on such factors as its overall objectives relative to computing, the organization's overall management control philosophy, and the sophistication of line management as computer users.

Limitations of a Cost Allocation Approach

Charging schemes are frequently regarded primarily as mechanisms for allocating the costs of the computer center among users in some equitable manner. Cost allocation is indeed one function of charging; in particular, it ensures that computing costs are taken into account in management information used for evaluation and decision making. However, viewing charging purely as a cost allocation mechanism fails to recognize that charges have a direct influence on user attitudes, behavior, and decisions, and that the main motivation underlying charging is usually to control computing activities through this influence on users. Charging will only be fully effective if these underlying management control objectives are explicitly considered in designing the charge-out system, so as to ensure that the desired influence does in fact occur.

Computing possesses several important characteristics as a resource which complicate the charge-out problem and, in particular, make it unlikely that a charge-out system designed purely from the viewpoint of cost allocation will yield the benefits that are potentially available. Specifically:

> Due to the *economic characteristics of computer costs*—in particular the high proportion of fixed and joint costs and the presence of economies of scale— the true "cost" of a specific computer task cannot be clearly defined. Fairly arbitrary allocation decisions are required in setting prices; "equity" does not provide an operationally useful criterion for making these pricing decisions—they can only be made in relation to the objectives to be achieved. In the process, implicit costs such as the opportunity cost of idle capacity have to be considered as well as explicit accounting costs.

> Because of the *long-run nature of most computing expenditure decisions,* charge-out policies must take into account not only the immediate desire to promote cost-effective use of resources, but also the long-term strategic considerations associated with computing.

> Because of the *technical complexity involved in measuring resource usage,* the desire for accuracy must be balanced against cost considerations and

against the need to make charges controllable by, and understandable to, the user.

With the *variety of users and applications* typically associated with a large installation, a degree of market segmentation is likely to be necessary in setting prices; a single uniform charging structure is unlikely to be universally appropriate.

The *significance of computer charges* in many users' budgets can make them highly sensitive to these charges. Factors such as the basis used for setting prices and the extent to which users feel able to control their charges can be of critical importance.

The *presence of competition* in the form of small departmental facilities and outside services may have to be taken into account in designing the charging structure in order to encourage the desired distribution of expenditure among these alternatives. The problem may also be complicated by sale of services to outside customers for which the pricing objectives are likely to be rather different.

These complexities have two important consequences. First, traditional cost accounting techniques alone do not provide enough guidance in designing a computer charge-out system to act as an effective management control tool. For example, as we show in Chapter 4, the sophisticated pricing techniques employed by commercial service bureaus, such as output-related pricing, quantity discounts, and surcharges for use of specialized software, can also be usefully employed within an internal charging scheme, even though the ultimate objectives associated with commercial and internal pricing are rather different. Yet the potential value of these techniques is only apparent if one thinks in terms of their influence on user behavior; they seem quite irrelevant from the viewpoint of simple cost allocation.

A second consequence is that principles inherent in the cost allocation approach, such as full cost recovery and equitable charging, are not necessarily appropriate where the objective is to promote efficiency and effectiveness.[4] Consider, for example, cost recovery policy in the case when demand does not match capacity. Since computer capacity can generally only be changed in large increments, periods of over- or underutilization are bound to occur as a result of configuration changes or fluctuations in demand. If a cost recovery policy is rigidly adhered to, prices are driven up during periods of underutilization, thus further reduc-

[4]Legal requirements may limit an organization's freedom to diverge from these principles. A particular case is the federal policy requiring that charges for government contract work be based on rates designed to recover the full cost of the installation, and applied on an equal basis to both government-funded and other users. This policy can act as a severe constraint on the organization's ability to manipulate prices in the interests of effectiveness and efficiency. For a further discussion of this problem, see H. Kanter, A. Moore and N. Singer, "The Allocation of Computer Time by University Computer Centers," *Journal of Business*, vol. 41, no. 3 (July 1968), pp. 373–384.

ing demand, while the opposite effect occurs during overutilization.[5] It may be preferable to accept a temporary revenue deficit or surplus (charging this against general organizational overhead) where this will bring usage more closely into line with capacity and maintain stability of prices.

A further example occurs in the design of a charging scheme. The key objective in designing a price structure should be to produce charges that will have the desired influence on users; though equity will obviously be a major consideration in pricing, it should not be the central one. Computer charging schemes are often made very complex in order to achieve great accuracy in measuring users' resource consumption. Such complexity is expensive and often leads to charges that are incomprehensible to the user; the accuracy obtained is of value only to the extent that it is likely to materially affect users' decisions, and to the extent that the resulting improvement in effectiveness and efficiency justifies the cost involved.

[5]Kanter, Moore and Singer, op. cit.

3 / POLICY-LEVEL ISSUES

This chapter is concerned with issues that arise in determining the basic structure of a charge-out system. First we discuss the question of when charging is worthwhile. We then examine alternative approaches in two key areas: budgeting for computing, and financial control of the computer facility.

To Charge or Not to Charge

Cost of Charge-Out Systems. Any charge-out system is likely to be expensive to operate. Billing is normally carried out through computer routines that keep track of each task's usage of system resources, generate charges for each job and report these to the user, and produce monthly accounting summaries; these routines themselves consume system resources.[1] In addi-

[1] An indication of the level of overhead involved is provided by Nielsen, who describes a charging system in use at Stanford University as requiring

tion, there is a cost, both to the computer center and to users, in the administrative effort required for budgeting, opening and closing charge accounts, dealing with refund claims resulting from processing errors, and similar procedures.

In addition to these obvious costs, charging, like any control mechanism, is prone to dysfunctional side effects. In other words, due to the imperfections inevitable in any practicable system of control, there are bound to be cases where charging induces counterproductive behavior.[2] These dysfunctions can be minimized through careful design and management of the charge-out system, but they will never be entirely eliminated.

One particular difficulty arises from the fact that, while the costs of a computer facility are relatively fixed, the charge-out system presents them to users as variable costs dependent on resource usage. While this is obviously a basic characteristic of charge-out, it can also be a significant cause of dysfunctions in that user efforts to reduce or avoid charges may not be reflected in actual cost savings at the computer facility, and may therefore be counterproductive from the point of view of the organization. As a specific example, whenever an installation is left with spare capacity because potential

---

less than one percent of the system's CPU cycles (see N. R. Nielsen, "Flexible Pricing—An Approach to the Allocation of Computer Resources," *Proceedings AFIPS Fall Joint Computer Conference, 1968,* p. 531). Note also that the resource usage information produced for charging purposes is also of considerable value in installation management (see Chapter 5).

[2]For a general discussion of dysfunctional effects in control systems, see E. E. Lawler, III and J. G. Rhode, *Information and Control in Organizations* (Santa Monica: Goodyear Publishing Co., 1976).

users do not have the requisite budget available or because they are not prepared to pay the normal process-. ing charges, there is an opportunity cost to the organization.[3] Such problems may be avoidable through sufficient flexibility in budgeting and pricing and, where appropriate, through sales to external users. Nevertheless, it is not uncommon in practice to come across situations where a machine sits idle while there are users able and willing to utilize the spare resources, but inhibited from doing so by the charging policy.

Against all these costs must be balanced the more effective and efficient use of resources associated with improved managerial control. As Nielsen says:

> It is true that pricing does result in more administrative work, but pricing also provides for better utilization of the available resources. While the computer may not perform any additional processing for users, the processing it does perform is more valuable to the organization. Thus the system is doing more valuable computing even if it is not doing more computing. So although pricing does involve additional costs, it returns additional benefits.[4]

Thus, the appropriateness of charging in any particular context must be judged in terms of the extent to which the benefits obtained are likely to justify the costs involved.

[3]This cost may not be as great as it initially appears. A reduced work load improves the speed of service provided by the installation, and the value of this improvement to users may partially, if not fully, offset the opportunity cost of the unused capacity. In fact, beyond a certain level of capacity utilization, the value of any increased usage is liable to be more than offset by the cost of the increased congestion produced.

[4]Norman R. Nielsen, "The Allocation of Computing Resources—Is Pricing the Answer?" *Communications of the ACM*, vol. 13, no. 8 (August 1970), p. 473.

When Charging Is Justified. Broadly speaking, the need for charging grows with the scale and complexity of an organization's computing activities.[5] When an organization is in the early stages of computer use, computing expenditures are likely to be relatively insignificant and the potential payoff from charging correspondingly small. Management will generally be concerned more with promoting than regulating computer usage, and charging may be felt to discourage experimentation with new applications.[6] Moreover, a charge-out system relies for its effectiveness on users making informed decisions within the framework of the computer pricing and budgeting mechanisms; with a relatively unsophisticated user community, it may be desirable to retain central control over computing activities.

As computer use grows within the organization, controls become necessary to allocate capacity and to ensure its efficient use. The normal initial approach is direct administrative control by a central steering committee and/or the computer center itself. These mechanisms may continue to be adequate as long as the level of computing expenditures remains relatively small, the range of applications limited, and the pressures on the computer center manageable. Generally, however,

[5]Further discussion on this topic will be found in R. L. Nolan, *Management Accounting and Control of Data Processing* (National Association of Accountants, June 1977).

[6]There are dangers in this short-term viewpoint. With computer services freely available, users are liable to develop wasteful habits and become committed to applications that may not be cost-effective. This may lead to problems with users when it becomes necessary to assert control at a later stage.

24

there comes a point where direct controls alone become inadequate. This may be indicated by symptoms such as the following:

> The computer center is continuously overloaded. Additions to capacity simply produce corresponding increases in demand. Management is alarmed at the escalation in computing expenditures, and is concerned that the resources are not being employed cost-effectively.

> Users are finding that computing plays an increasingly important role in their activities, and are frustrated with their lack of control over this area.

> Management sees an increasing need to ensure that line managers become involved in the computing activities associated with their areas of responsibility and to make them accountable for these activities.

This is the point at which charging is likely to be justified.

Scope of the Charge-Out System. The introduction of charging provides a powerful new control mechanism. However, while this reduces the burden on, and the need for, direct administrative controls, it is unlikely to completely replace them. In every aspect of controlling computing, there is a choice between using direct controls and regulating through charge-out. For example, a central steering committee can be used to decide what applications will be developed, or this can be left to the discretion of user departments within the constraints of their available funds. Similarly, at the operational level, scheduling of jobs may be carried out according to fixed criteria or controlled by the computer center management, or, alternatively, may be determined through the action of a priority-pricing scheme. Again, efficient utilization of resources can be pursued through restrictions on program run time and memory occupancy, disc quotas, etc., or through manipulation of the resource pricing scheme.

Both approaches have their advantages and disadvantages. Direct controls tend to be cheaper, more straightforward, and more predictable in their action. On the other hand, because charge-out exercises control indirectly through economic incentives, this approach leaves users with a greater degree of autonomy in their computing activities. Moreover, control through charge-out is a more flexible method. For example, printing of large volumes of output during prime time can be discouraged through time-of-day-related differentials in printing charges; this approach still allows the user who badly needs large volume, prime-time output to obtain it at a price. The alternative direct approach—a rule that defers all large volume output for overnight printing—either applies indiscriminately to all users, or requires a cumbersome administrative apparatus to cater for exceptions.

As a result of these tradeoffs, organizations typically rely on a combination of charge-out and direct controls to manage their computing activities, choosing the mix that seems most appropriate for the circumstances involved. When charging is first introduced in an organization, the charge-out system may initially play a limited role with management retaining direct control over many key decision areas. For example, a "funny-money" charging scheme may be used to ration computer usage with the basic decisions on the allocation of computing funds still being made centrally. Or users may be charged for processing operations but not for system development work, the latter being controlled centrally through a computer policy committee. Experience shows, however, that as the scale and complexity of computer usage continues to grow, central regulation becomes increasingly difficult, and the pressures grow to decentralize responsibility for computing activities within the organization. Thus, the role of charge-out tends to expand as an organization moves through the stages of growth in computer usage.[7]

Even when the charge-out system plays the central role, it is still likely to be supplemented with direct controls. In some cases, direct controls may be considered necessary where the market mechanism does not produce the desired incentives. For example, many organizations are unwilling to give users freedom to choose between internal and external sources of computing on the basis of relative costs, on the grounds that decisions made on this basis do not take account of the interest of the organization as a whole in maintaining a large, fully utilized central computer facility. In other cases, direct control may be viewed as more cost-effec-

[7]See R. L. Nolan, *Management Accounting and Control of Data Processing* (National Association of Accountants, June 1977).

tive than control through the pricing and budgeting mechanisms. For example, where it is desired to reduce the number of long program runs submitted during peak periods, direct limits on job size may provide a far cheaper and more straightforward method of control than incorporating a premium rate for large jobs into the charging structure, while the loss of flexibility produced may be relatively unimportant.

Free Service Classes. A particular case where control through charge-out is not worthwhile occurs when there are specific categories within the overall pattern of computer use where the potential benefits from charging individual users do not justify the costs involved. This may occur, for example, where the class of work involved has very low resource requirements, or where resource usage would not be significantly influenced by charging. Where such categories occur and can be clearly defined, it is generally preferable to establish them as free service classes. Rather than billing individual users, charges for these classes should be allocated to an appropriate organizational overhead account—ideally, at the point in the organization that controls access to the free service.

Examples of services that might be provided free in this way are occasional ad hoc inquiries from a corporate data base or small-scale jobs run in background mode during off-peak periods. A particular case in the university environment is small-scale student computing. The level of resource usage for instruction-related student computing is generally quite low, while the effort involved in setting up, administering, and billing student accounts for each course can be considerable. It may be preferable to eliminate direct charging of students, or set up student-oriented classes of use such as small compile-and-go Fortran program runs as free service classes; direct restrictions on program size, run time, etc., can be used to restrict individual students' resource usage where necessary. One example of such a policy is that operated at Dartmouth College. Dartmouth has concluded that only a small minority of students are likely to make unjustifiably large use of computer resources under a free-use policy. It has, therefore, adopted such a policy, exercising control over excessive demand through software arrangements that restrict the total resources that can be consumed by any one student.[8]

Alternative Approaches to Budgeting

Purpose of the Budgeting Process. The computing budget normally covers the same one-year cycle as the organization's overall financial budget, though the two budgeting processes may be only partially integrated. When computing is charged out to users, computer budgeting must be carried out in two dimensions: expenditure and revenue. The expenditure budget is a line-oriented budget for the computer facility; it defines the planned total cost of the facility, and breaks

[8]See A. W. Luehrmann and J. M. Nevison, "Computer Use Under a Free-Access Policy," *Science,* vol. 184, 1974, pp. 957–961.

these costs down into responsibility centers and re-source categories to provide a basis for internal control of the facility. The revenue budget, on the other hand, is broken down by user area and defines each organiza-tional unit's planned usage of computing resources, along with any planned revenue from external users; this latter budget provides the basis for controlling computer usage through the charging mechanism. In general, system development activities and on-going operations will be budgeted for through separate pro-cesses—at least on the revenue side.

The computing budget is of key significance to all those concerned with the organization's computing ac-tivities—top management, the management of the computer facility, and computer users. For top man-agement the budget defines the planned level of ex-penditures on computing resources, and also defines the planned distribution of resource usage within the organization. From the viewpoint of the computer fa-cility management, the budget establishes the level of funding available to support the facility and the scale of demand that will have to be met.[9] Finally, for each user the budget provides an indication of the computing resources that will be available to it.

The end product of any computer budgeting pro-

[9]In general, the level of demand is expressed simply in terms of the total value of services to be provided; the computer facility then uses its own judgment in its internal planning to assess the likely distribution of demand between the various categories of service (batch processing, time-sharing, system development, data storage, etc.). However, where management needs a more reliable basis for planning and controlling the distribution of demand—for example, between two machines operated at the same facility —the revenue budget can be broken down to provide this.

cess must always be a pair of consistent expenditure and revenue budgets (allowing for any planned surplus or deficit of revenue over expenditure). However, the process by which these budgets are established, and thus the role played by the various participants in making the basic allocation decisions embodied in the budget, can vary considerably. The key variable here is the extent to which users are left free to choose the level of their computing expenditures. The alternatives of fully centralized and fully decentralized budgeting are discussed below; we then point to some ways of compromising between these two extremes. Finally, discussed is another important variable in the budgeting process—the extent to which users are left free to allocate their computing expenditures between central and noncentral resources. The discussion deals primarily with the problem of budgeting for operations, but many of the same general considerations apply equally to budgeting for system development.

Centralized Budgeting. Under a fully centralized budgeting procedure, the basic decisions on the overall level of computing expenditure and the internal allocation of computing resources are made centrally by top management or through a computer steering committee on which all interested parties are represented. The allocation is established by distributing the total planned provision of resources among users in the form of "computer units" that can be exchanged for computer services. (The total budget allocated may be slightly higher than the revenue target to allow for the fact that budgets will not be fully spent.) Though generally expressed in dollar terms, the computer allocations can normally only be spent at the computer center and are therefore commonly referred to as "funny money."

A highly simplified diagrammatic representation of the budgeting process is shown in Figure 3.1. It will be seen that with this approach, computing expenditures are treated as an overhead cost in the organization's financial budget structure; user departments' operating budgets make no direct provision for computing charges. Once the overall computing budget has been established, the process of allocating "funny-money" computing budgets to departments and generating charges against these budgets is entirely independent of the organization's financial system.

With a centralized budgeting process the role of the charge-out system in influencing resource allocation is strictly limited. "Funny-money" charging acts primarily as a rationing mechanism. Moreover, provided the computer allocations are reasonably restrictive, it will encourage users to make cost-effective use of resources by forcing them to make tradeoffs between alternative uses of their allocations, for example, in selecting applications, technical strategies, and priority levels.[10] However, since,

---

[10]The proviso is important: if a user's allocation is too generous, he will have no incentive to be selective in his choice of applications or to reduce his charges by careful use of resources. One computer center director complained that his users failed to take advantage of off-peak discounts. On investigation, the cause was found to be that users had quite enough budget to do all their computing at premium rates!

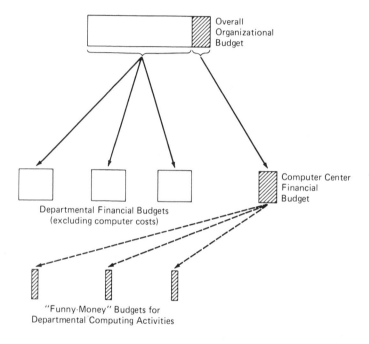

Figure 3.1. Simplified representation of a centralized budgeting process for computing

under a "funny-money" budgeting arrangement, users have no direct means of trading off computer use against other expenditures, computing remains an essentially free resource for users in the sense that it involves no sacrifice in other areas. While this encourages experimentation with new computing applications, it does nothing to restrict the level of computing resources demanded by user departments; it is left to the central allocation committee to attempt to balance effectively the conflicting demands of different user departments, and the demands of computing in general against other forms of expenditure. Thus, under a centralized budgeting process, the charge-out system plays no role in the fundamental decisions on the scale and distribution of computer usage within the organization; these decisions are retained at the policy-making level, and the charge-out system simply provides a mechanism for implementing them in environments, such as job-shop or time-shared computing, where some form of rationing is needed.

Decentralized Budgeting. The charging mechanism plays a far more central role when computing is budgeted for on a decentralized basis. This approach is depicted (again, in highly simplified form) in Figure 3.2. Here, internal computer charges are treated on the same basis as "real" cash expenditures as far as user departments are concerned; departmental operating budgets include a provision for computing costs, so that users establish their computing allocations within the organization's normal financial budgeting framework.

34

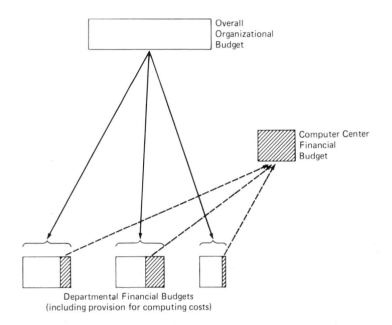

Figure 3.2. Simplified representation of a decentralized budgeting process for computing

The aggregate of individual departments' provisions for computing implicitly defines the computer facility's expected internal revenue; this, together with anticipated external revenues and any deficit or surplus negotiated with senior management, then defines the facility's expenditure budget.

Note that, in contrast to the centralized approach, the computing budget is here established through a bottom-up rather than a top-down process. The basic sequence of steps is reversed: rather than establishing the computer expenditure budget and then from this developing a revenue budget, the latter is established first and the expenditure budget derived from it.

There are important differences between the centralized and decentralized approaches. Under a decentralized approach user departments have full control over their computing expenditures within the constraints of their overall operating budgets. While this decentralization of responsibility can bring major benefits, it also relies on users exercising their control effectively. This involves, for example, proper user understanding of the considerations involved in effective use of computing, reporting systems that clearly identify and break down computer costs within users' budgets, and performance evaluation procedures that explicitly focus on managers' effectiveness in using computing.[11]

Computer center management is also greatly

[11]Further discussion of these considerations will be found in R. L. Nolan, *Management Accounting and Control of Data Processing*, (National Association of Accountants, June 1977).

affected by the budgeting procedure used. Under a centralized allocation procedure, the computer center's task essentially is to provide the greatest possible quantity and quality of computer services at a predetermined level of funding. On the other hand, when user departments are given direct control of their computing expenditure, the computer center faces an internal "market" for is services, and thus has a much more entrepreneurial role. Computer center management has considerable autonomy in choosing the scale and type of computing capacity to be provided but must generate sufficient revenue to support this capacity (taking into account any agreed surplus or deficit); thus, the task now entails not just management of costs, but also management of demand. This involves taking account of demand elasticities in setting prices,[12] and may also require external selling of services to make up shortfalls in revenue.

Given the difficulties involved in adjusting computer center capacity and costs from year to year, the center will need to take measures to reduce the uncertainty in future demand. Involving users in long-term planning for computing and encouraging long-term supply contracts with major users can be important

[12]Experience at the Massachusetts Institute of Technology in the early '70s showed that users there reacted typically to a price change in one of two ways: either they continued at their previous level of expenditure, altering their consumption accordingly, or they maintained their previous consumption, accepting the associated change in expenditure. The MIT Computer Center's revenue appeared to divide roughly equally between the two categories, so that a ten percent change in computing rates produced a five percent change in revenues, and a roughly equal opposite change in resource usage.

tools in this area. The computer center's task of matching supply and demand will be greatly eased if some flexibility is provided in its cost recovery target. For example, a long-term recovery goal may be adopted, permitting carry-over of a limited deficit or surplus (e.g., up to 10 percent of a year's budget) from one year to the next.

From the viewpoint of senior management, the most important difference between the centralized and decentralized approaches lies in the elimination of a negotiation process for establishing the allocation of resources to computing and among computer users, and its replacement with a market mechanism that establishes this allocation implicitly through the decisions of individual user groups. In theory, given suitable computer pricing, a decentralized budgeting process in which users trade off computing against alternative forms of expenditure will produce a cost-effective allocation of resources to computing and between users, working in the manner of Adam Smith's "invisible hand."[13] Thus, again in theory, management should be able to decentralize control over the scale and distribution of computer usage with confidence that the financial budgeting process will produce the "correct" allocation.

However, the problem is rather more complicated in practice. Real-world computer pricing schemes and budgeting processes are far from perfect economic

[13] See S. Smidt, "The Use of Hard and Soft Money Budgets, and Prices to Limit Demand for a Centralized Computer Facility," *Proceedings AFIPS Fall Joint Computer Conference, 1968,* pp. 499–509.

mechanisms. Moreover, purely economic criteria are not necessarily appropriate to these fundamental allocation decisions. These considerations are reflected in the doubts often expressed regarding the ability of a decentralized budgeting procedure to produce the right allocation of resources.[14] For example, it is pointed out that management's policy objectives with respect to computing may go beyond a straightforward concern for cost-effectiveness. Furthermore, there is often a feeling—particularly in nonprofit institutions— that the spending power of individual organizational units does not necessarily correspond to the value of their activities to the organization; this feeling is reflected, for example, in the common objection that "rich" departments or projects will gain at the expense of "poor" ones under a decentralized budgeting arrangement. In addition, it is sometimes suggested that, because of special characteristics associated with computing, line managers' decisions on computer use will not always reflect its true costs and benefits in relation to other expenditures; this concern appears in statements such as "departmental managers do not appreciate the potential value of computing and need to be encouraged to use it," or "line managers are only concerned with short-term results and will not be interested in computer projects that have long-term payoffs."

Since there is no objective way to assess the validity

[14] See, for example, the discussion of centralized versus decentralized budgeting in S. Gill and P. A. Samet, "Charging for Computer Time in Universities," *Computer Bulletin*, vol. 13, no. 1, (January 1969), pp. 14–16.

and importance of such objections to decentralized budgeting, its acceptability in practice often depends on how far management feels the results would be consistent with its own view of the correct scale and distribution of computing expenditures. Our own opinion is that a decentralized budgeting process will generally produce better allocation decisions than can be produced centrally, provided adequate measures are taken to help and encourage line management to exercise their control over computing effectively. Moreover, as we have already indicated, decentralization has important side benefits in bringing the allocation process within the organization's normal budgetary framework—thereby eliminating the extra political tensions inherent in a special computer allocation process, encouraging line managers to involve themselves more closely in their departments' computing activities, and greatly increasing the computer center's incentive to remain efficient and responsive to user needs. It is true that a decentralized allocation process has its imperfections; however, the real issue is the importance of these imperfections relative to all the disadvantages associated with a centralized approach.[15] It should also be pointed out that decentralization of the budgeting process still allows management to exercise some degree of central control where it wishes to influence users' decisions, both through manipulation of the

[15] This point is well made in a report discussing a proposed change from centralized to decentralized budgeting at the University of Rochester. See D. Goldstein, M. C. Jensen and D. Smith, *Report of the President's Committee on Computing Problems and Opportunities,* University of Rochester, 1973, pp. 1–10.

pricing scheme (e.g., subsidizing all or certain types of computer use from central funds) and through direct restrictions of various kinds.

Hybrid Approaches. The centralized and decentralized budgeting arrangements described above really represent the extremes in a spectrum of possible arrangements with varying degrees of decentralization. Described below are some of the ways in which organizations may compromise between the two basic approaches.

One important variable determining the degree of decentralization is the organizational level at which budgetary decisions are taken. Even under a "funny-money" budgeting scheme, some degree of decentralization can be introduced by making bulk computer allocations to the major organizational subunits and allowing the managers of these subunits to distribute their allocations within their area of responsibility; this retains central control over the basic tradeoff decisions between computing resources and other expenditures, but allows intermediate levels of the organization more discretion over their internal distribution than would be the case if "funny-money" allocations were made directly to individual projects or users.

Where charges are treated as "real money" and charged against operating budgets, budgetary control may be exercised at a higher level than that of the smallest individual budgetary units. For example, in a university, the allocation of funds to computing activities might be made by the deans of each school, and for administrative computing by the chief administrative officer; the distribution of resources would then be controlled centrally within each of these major subunits. Often it will be appropriate to assign budgetary responsibility for different types of computing activity at different levels. For example, in an airline company the reservation system might be funded centrally and charged to an overhead account, while systems with more narrowly defined functions, such as parts control and crew scheduling, are charged to the appropriate departments.

Another form of compromise between the centralized and decentralized approaches is the mixing of "funny-money" and "real-money" charges. For example:

> Some types of resource may be charged for on a "funny-money" basis and others charged directly against operating budgets. For example, it is very common to find centrally provided services charged for in "funny-money" terms, while other forms of computing are treated as "real" cash expenditures. Even within the central facility, variable cost items such as documentation and punched cards may be charged as real expenditures, even though the main fixed-cost resources are allocated on a "funny-money" basis.

> "Real-money" budgets and charges may be used for some classes of use or user, while "funny-money" allocations are provided for others. An obvious example of this approach occurs in universities, where

instructional computing is often funded through "funny-money" allocations, while computing for funded research and administrative applications is charged against financial budgets. A potential difficulty with this type of arrangement is preventing the use of "funny-money" allocations for purposes that are supposed to be paid for in "real money."

A basic central allocation of "funny money" may be made, but this allocation deliberately kept well short of users' full requirements. User areas then supplement their allocations as desired with "real money" from their operating budgets. This mechanism can be used to indirectly subsidize computing and to provide the computer center with some stability of income, while still obtaining the benefits of users trading off computing against other expenditures at the margin.

Other forms of compromise between the two approaches are also possible. For example, an organization may control its computing resource allocation decisions centrally, but may nevertheless include users' allocations of computing funds as a line item in their operating budgets. This ensures that computer costs are reflected in internal performance measures and other management information, and encourages line managers to be aware of these costs, even though they have no direct control over them. As another example, an organization may use decentralized budgeting to determine the internal allocation of computing resources, but may retain central control over the overall level of computing expenditures. Obviously, any given organization must select the solution that best fits its own particular circumstances.

Treatment of Noncentral Resources. The discussion so far has dealt with one dimension of decentralization in the budgeting process, that is, the extent to which users are free to choose the level of their computing expenditures. Another important dimension is users' degree of freedom to direct these expenditures as they wish—for example, toward their own minicomputer installation or purchase of outside computer services—rather than having to use the central facility exclusively. It should be emphasized that these are largely independent dimensions. Although "funny-money" allocation schemes typically cover only the services of the central facility, there is no reason why they should not be extended to include all forms of computer services. Similarly, while charging for computing in terms of "real money" greatly increases users' pressures to be allowed to purchase their computer services from what they regard as the most cost-effective source, such freedom does not necessarily have to be granted.

The key issue in deciding on the treatment of noncentral resources is the same as that discussed earlier: what arrangement is likely to produce an effective allocation of resources—in this case between central, distributed, and external sources of computing. Under a "funny-money" allocation scheme that covers only central services, users have little incentive to seek more cost-effective sources than the computer center (since the former must be paid for from operating funds—if this is even permitted—while the latter are effectively free); thus, the organization is unlikely to take full advantage of alternatives such as minicomputers and resource-sharing networks. On the other hand, if users are given freedom to choose where they spend their computer allocations, the question arises how far their choices, based on the relative costs to them of central and noncentral sources, will be consistent with the organization's overall interests. The same question obviously also arises under a decentralized "real-money" budgeting arrangement.

As will be shown in the next chapter, the computer center's pricing scheme can to some extent be designed to encourage users to make a cost-effective choice between central and noncentral services. Nevertheless, many organizations are unwilling to rely completely on the market mechanism and therefore restrict users in their choice of source. This may be done, for example, by requiring central approval of any computer-related expenditures other than for central services. Alternatively, even stronger control may be exercised by giving the central computer department responsibility for supplying all forms of computing resources, including minicomputers and outside services.

As with the previously discussed issue of centralized versus decentralized budgeting, management must decide the degree of freedom it will allow users over their source of supply in relation to its overall policy goals for computing and its general management control philosophy. We would point out, however, that whatever the potential dangers of misallocation associated with allowing users freedom in this area, it does bring with it the important benefits associated with decentralization in general: elimination of a cumbersome and conflict-inducing central control process, increase of line management's accountability for all aspects of their computing activities, and reinforcement of the market pressures acting on the computer center.

Financial Control Options

Cost-based versus Profit-based Control. There are two main approaches available for controlling the computer facility. When it operates largely independently of outside competition, pricing of its services and control of its performance must be based on the facility's detailed cost and revenue budgets, and on comparison of actuals against budgets. Alternatively, where the facility competes on a significant scale for inside and/or outside business, prices will be governed by market forces, and control can be based on its overall profitability as a independent division or subsidiary.

Under the first approach the facility is typically set up as an internal cost center.[16] In many simple charg-

[16]One sometimes finds the computer center set up as a profit center even though it is not subject to the constraints of external competition. In our view, such an arrangement has little value: the center's management cannot safely be given the freedom normally associated with a profit center, since it is a monopoly position with respect to its users; if, on the other hand, its profit-seeking behavior is constrained—for example, by imposing a break-even profit target—this effectively puts it in the same position as a cost center. The profit center arrangement is sometimes adopted on the grounds

ing schemes, costs are allocated retrospectively, based on each previous month's actual costs and usage; however, this approach has serious drawbacks from the viewpoint of management control: charging rates fluctuate from month to month with the overall volume of usage, severely weakening users' ability to budget for and control their charges effectively. Charging rates should therefore be set at the beginning of each year on the basis of planned costs and resource usage (in other words, charges are based on standard rather than actual costs); this provides users with a predictable, stable basis for planning and control.

With standard cost-based pricing, any deviations from the plans used as a basis for rate setting will appear as an under- or overrecovery of costs by the computer center, which can then be analyzed to determine the extent to which it is due to volume, cost, or efficiency variances; such analysis provides a powerful tool for management control of the center.[17] Where a component of the deficit or surplus can be directly attributed to a particular user department, it may be appropriate to assign it to that user's budget; the remaining deficit or surplus may be handled by charging

---

that this allows market-oriented pricing techniques such as off-peak discounts, long-term bulk supply rates, etc. However, there is no reason why the same techniques cannot be applied within a cost center framework.

[17]Volume variances are those attributable to differences between actual and planned output (i.e., usage) volumes; cost variances are those due to differences between the actual *unit* costs of input resources (e.g., machine rentals, supplies prices, wage rates, etc.) and those assumed in budgeting; efficiency variances are those related to differences between actual and plan in the ratio of inputs to outputs (e.g., more operators needed than expected for a given installation work load).

it to general overhead or by carrying it forward to be recovered in the next period.[18]

The second alternative, in which the facility is set up as a profit center or subsidiary that competes against other suppliers, is growing increasingly popular, particularly with large corporations.[19] Competition provides a strong spur to high quality performance and responsiveness to user needs at the computer center. Moreover, the arrangement provides management with a direct measure of the center's performance—namely, its profitability.[20] On the other hand, profit maximizing behavior on the part of the computer center will only be consistent with the organization's overall interests if users are sufficiently sophisticated to effectively protect

[18]Many computer centers handle variances by allocating them among users on some pro rata basis, or by making midyear rate adjustments designed to correct any deficit or surplus. Such corrective efforts seem to have little value, since they will not eliminate the cause of the original variance. Moreover, they have the disadvantage that they create uncertainty for users, weakening their ability to effectively budget for and control computer costs, and undermining their view of the facility as a business-oriented operation. Retrospective adjustments may be particularly troublesome for users where they are formally prohibited from exceeding their budgetary provisions. Where the center is required to break even as a matter of policy, the need for price adjustments can be avoided by allowing deficits or surpluses to be carried over from one accounting period to the next; this also eliminates another dysfunctional practice common in computer centers—that of speeding up or slowing down expenditures toward the end of a fiscal year, again in an effort to match expenses and revenues.

[19]See R. L. Nolan, *Management Accounting and Control of Data Processing,* (National Association of Accountants, June 1977).

[20]In some organizations where the computer center does not actively compete with outside suppliers, the test of the market is applied by directly setting charging ranges at a level corresponding to external market prices (the latter being assessed through a survey of comparable commercial services). This again allows control of the center on the basis of profitability. The arrangement does, however, depend on the existence of commercial services that are directly comparable with those offered by the center.

their interests in an arm's-length buyer-seller relationship with the center; where these conditions are not satisfied, there is a danger that the profit incentive may result in less effective use of computers in the organization.

An important issue under both the cost-center and profit-center approaches is the composition of the costs which the computer facility is required to recover (or earn a profit on). Decisions regarding the inclusion of cost components such as organizational overhead charges or hardware depreciation costs can significantly affect price calculations and hence the level of users' charges. In a "real money" budgeting environment, this will, in turn, influence the competitiveness of the computer center's services relative to alternative sources of computing. This consideration may be important even when users' freedom to select alternative sources is restricted, since rates which users regard as uncompetitive will still generate dissatisfaction with the center and strong pressures for permission to go elsewhere.

It is important that the basis used in establishing the computer center's costs is comparable with that used in representing the costs of alternatives. For example, a proportion of general overhead is often allocated to the computer center, so that the rates it charges reflect this allocation of overhead as well as the direct costs of the center. On the other hand, alternatives such as a local minicomputer installation or use of a service bureau may be included in users' budgets at their basic direct cost. Such a discrepancy in treatment will bias users against employing the central services even when these would in practice be more cost-effective. In one large corporation, the corporate data center instituted a charging scheme which involved recovery of a share of corporate overhead in addition to its direct costs. The divisional data centers' cost recovery targets, on the other hand, did not include any allocation of corporate overhead. The resulting rate differentials caused a major shift of usage away from the corporate center, even though the true costs to the organization of processing at this center were no higher than for the divisional centers.

Wholesale-Retail Schemes. [21] Wholesale-retail schemes are a recent innovation of considerable potential value to organizations with large-scale, diverse computing activities. Under such a scheme, the functions associated with production of computer services (i.e., running the data center) are separated from those associated with delivering these services to end users (i.e., providing user support, charging, etc.). The computer center (or centers) no longer deals directly with users; instead, it supplies its services on a bulk supply or "wholesale" basis to distributor organizations, which in turn "retail" these services to their local users. The "wholesaler" and

[21]Further discussion on this topic will be found in D. L. Grobstein and R. P. Uhlig, "A Wholesale-Retail Concept for Computer Network Management," *Proceedings AFIPS Fall Joint Computer Conference, 1972,* pp. 889–898, and in a paper by E. Stefferud presented at the ACM SIGMETRICS Technical Meeting on Pricing Computer Services, Nov. 20–21, 1975 and published in *Performance Evaluation Review,* vol. 5C, no. 1, March 1976, pp. 31–70.

"retailer" organizations are financially independent, dealing with each other on an arm's-length contractual basis.

Figure 3.3(a) illustrates the way such an arrangement can be used within an organization. Here a central computer facility supplies services in bulk to three organizational units. (Within a corporation these units might be divisions or functional units; within a university they might represent, for example, two schools of the university plus the administrative branch or, alternatively, three campuses in a multicampus institution.) Each organizational unit buys an overall volume of computer services from the central facility, and itself controls the way these services are distributed. Thus, each unit can tailor its handling of computing to its own particular needs and policies. In particular, each unit can make its own decisions on pricing, budgeting, and financial control of computing. For example, one unit might decide to provide computing free or at subsidized rates, a second to use a "funny-money" allocation scheme, and a third to budget and charge for its computing internally in "real money" terms. Furthermore, different units might employ quite different rate structures for charging users.

The advantages of distributing control in this way become particularly strong in more complex situations such as that shown in Figure 3.3(b), where there are several computer facilities, each shared between several units, and where the organization is also involved in buying and selling external services. Through the wholesale-retail scheme, issues relating to control of the

(a) *Single supplier*

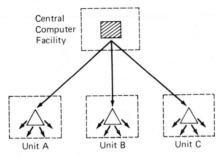

(b) *Multiple supplier*

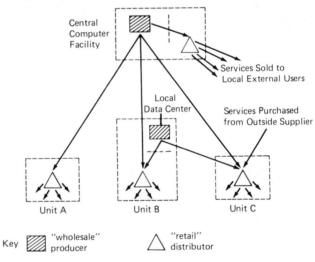

Figure 3.3. Illustrative wholesale-retail schemes for control of computing

computer centers, supply to external users, and allocation and use within the user subunits can be effectively separated. Each user subunit is able to handle its computing activities in the way it deems most effective, and is able to employ a single uniform pricing and budgeting framework, even though it obtains computer services from several different sources. This greatly simplifies what could otherwise be an extremely complex management problem.

4 / DESIGN OF A PRICING SCHEME

We now turn our attention to the central component of any charge-out system—the pricing scheme through which users' charges are calculated. We begin by outlining some basic principles underlying the design of a pricing scheme. The remainder of the chapter discusses the development of a basic resource-related price structure, alternative pricing methods, pricing of service priority, charging for systems and programming resources, and finally some special pricing problems.

Underlying Principles

Objectives in Pricing. It was pointed out in Chapter 1 that for the purposes of effective design, charging is best regarded as a control mechanism rather than simply as a cost allocation process. If charging is viewed as a control mechanism, it becomes clear that the key consideration in deciding the basis for calculating charges, and the level of charging rates, must be the likely effect on users' decisions.

The pricing scheme can influence users at several levels, including such areas as:

Deciding whether to implement a new computer application, or choosing between alternative applications

Choosing between use of the central installation or an outside resource

Balancing the use of computing and manual effort (for example, in a statistical analysis problem)

Deciding among technical strategies that differ in the mix of resources required (as, for example, in "fine tuning" a program's structure to optimize the balance between core size and input-output activity, or in choosing between a batch or an on-line approach to data input)

Deciding the frequency and volume of outputs (e.g., reports daily or once a week)

Deciding what priority to request when submitting a job, or what time of day to do time-sharing work

An ideal pricing scheme will always motivate users to act in a manner completely consistent with management's objectives in all areas where users have discretion over resource usage.[1] This ideal obviously cannot

---

[1]Users will obviously not necessarily have discretion in all the areas indicated above; where their discretion is limited, the range of considerations involved in pricing is correspondingly reduced. For example, under a

be achieved in practice. Nevertheless, in designing a pricing scheme its effect on user behavior needs to be considered explicitly; this will enhance the effectiveness of charging, and reduce the need to supplement the charge-out system with direct controls and restrictions on users. As will be clear from subsequent discussion, such an approach involves consciously *pricing*, rather than simply costing, services.

Relation of Prices to Costs. On the whole, computing resources will be used most cost-effectively if users' decisions are based on a price structure that accurately reflects costs. For example, a user's decision on whether to use the computer in a particular application will normally be based on his estimates of the costs and benefits involved. Since the "costs" are represented to the user in the form of his computing charges, these charges ideally should reflect the actual costs to the organization of the resources involved. Similarly, a user's choice between technical strategies involving

"funny-money" charging scheme, where budgeting is controlled centrally, computer center prices will influence users' resource usage decisions, but will not affect the overall level of their resource usage or the distribution of expenditures between central and alternative sources of computing; thus, while the detailed structure of computer resource prices is still a concern here, the absolute level of prices relative to other forms of expenditure and alternative sources of computing is not so critical (except insofar as computer charges provide cost information for management information purposes). Similarly, in an administrative data processing environment, where the computer center rather than the user controls the technical strategy used in programs and systems, the emphasis in pricing will be more on controlling users' overall demands for computer services than on regulating the detailed pattern of hardware resource usage. Many specific observations on pricing in this chapter may not be relevant in situations where charging does not influence behavior in the area concerned.

different mixes of resource usage would normally best be based on rates reflecting the relative cost of the various resources involved. It is clear, therefore, that the computer center's cost structure must be used as the basis for establishing prices.[2]

This does not, however, imply that the price structure must necessarily always reflect costs. There may be instances where deviations from a strict cost basis for pricing will lead to better use of resources or will better support policy objectives. Thus, pricing requires a flexible approach: strict considerations of cost need to be supplemented with subjective judgments as to what is most likely to yield desired results. In particular, the pricing scheme must take account of implicit economic costs, such as those associated with risk, scarcity, con-

---

[2]This begs the question of what constitutes "cost." Strictly speaking, the computer center costs relevant to any specific decision on resource usage are the marginal, or incremental, costs of the resources involved. For example, in deciding whether to implement a new computer application, the costs that need to be considered in relation to the anticipated benefits are the incremental costs of providing the computer center resources required for the new system. Thus, if users are to be led to make economically sound decisions on the basis of the computer center's charges, these charges need to reflect the incremental cost of the associated resources. It is difficult to clearly define incremental costs in this context—particularly since resource usage decisions have only a very indirect impact on actual costs. Nevertheless it is clear that the incremental costs of resources will not necessarily correspond to the average unit costs calculated through conventional cost accounting procedures. Specifically, given the economies of scale normally associated with computing, incremental costs will be lower than the prices required to fully recover the cost of the center; for example, the cost of upgrading hardware per unit of processing power added is normally lower than the unit cost of existing capacity. The implication of this argument— that economically sound internal pricing will normally require that the computer center be run at a loss—is somewhat controversial. Nevertheless, it should be recognized that a price structure designed to reflect full resource costs will not necessarily always provide the appropriate basis for guiding individual decisions on computer usage or expenditure allocation.

gestion, and unused resources, as well as explicit accounting costs.

The examples below illustrate some of the circumstances in which deviations from cost-based pricing may be justified. Further examples will appear throughout the chapter.

> *Deviations from cost may be advisable where computing policy does not follow strictly economic criteria.* Consider, for example, the case of a small college that decides, for prestige or other reasons, to maintain its own computer center even though its small scale implies a higher cost than the alternative of using outside resources. Under these circumstances it may be advisable to subsidize the computer center so as to bring internal charging rates down at least to a level comparable to outside rates; otherwise, users will continually complain of excessive internal charges and will whenever possible use other sources to the detriment of the organization as a whole. The subsidy payment here explicitly reflects the costs incurred by management's policy of maintaining an in-house computing capability.
>
> A further example is that of a university which wishes, for reasons of institutional policy, to boost the use of computing for instructional purposes. Special rates for instructional use, subsidized from a central fund, could be used to support this objective.
>
> *Special pricing arrangements can be used to encourage users to take actions that will benefit the*

organization as a whole. For example, it has already been pointed out that long-term commitments from major users can greatly reduce the risk of the computer center finding itself with insufficient or excess capacity through unanticipated fluctuations in demand. Discounts can be employed to induce users to make such commitments, in effect transferring the risk from the computer center to themselves.

Another example arises in experimentation with new technology or pioneering "state-of-the-art" applications. The experience gained from such activities potentially benefits the whole organization, but involves the initial users in considerable risk. It would be appropriate for the organization to promote experimentation by subsidizing these activities.

Prices may be manipulated to influence demand. As was pointed out in Chapter 2, because computer capacity cannot generally be changed easily except in large increments, it may sometimes be necessary to accept a deficit or surplus at the computer center (implying prices that reflect less or more than full cost) in order to match demand to the available capacity. An example is provided by Stanford University which at one point quadrupled the capacity of its computer center to allow for long-term growth. Because the new configuration was initially heavily underutilized, charges based on an apportionment of full cost would have been very high and would have discouraged demand in a situation calling for rapid growth in volume. Instead, Stanford deliberately set its rates based on full utilization of the installation, even though this meant subsidizing the center while usage expanded.

Pricing may also be used to regulate demand for a particular resource within an installation. For example, a situation analogous to the Stanford experience described above can arise with shared software and data bases whose usage is initially low but is expected to grow with time. Where such resources are explicitly charged for, it would be reasonable to set prices at the level expected to prevail in the long-term when usage has expanded, even though at the low level of initial usage, costs would not be recovered.[3]

As another example—this time dealing with insufficient rather than excess capacity—an installation might face a temporary shortage of disc storage space while waiting for demand to grow sufficiently to justify installing another storage unit. During this period, it may be necessary to introduce a temporary surcharge for disc usage (recognizing the temporary scarcity value of the resource) in order to ration the available capacity.

Pricing may also be used to shift demand from one resource to another. It is common for one resource to be a bottleneck in an installation while

[3]If a large deficit is unacceptable to the organization, it can be amortized over several future periods and, if necessary, recovered in future charges.

others are relatively underutilized; for example, throughput may be limited by input-output capacity, leaving the remainder of the installation resource—core, central processor, etc.—relatively idle. This situation can be corrected by weighting the price structure heavily toward input-output to reflect the fact that it is usage of this resource that has the primary impact on hardware requirements, thereby encouraging users to reduce their usage of this resource (for example, by shifting tables, arrays, etc., from disc to main memory).

Pricing of services to external users may have to take account of market factors as well as costs. The organization's objective in pricing services to external users of its computing resources may be to maximize the net financial contribution provided by these users rather than simply to charge them an equitable proportion of costs. The price structure that maximizes the contribution obtained from external usage may bear no relation to costs. For example, where the computer center possesses resources such as a specialized software package not readily available elsewhere, the optimum price for use of these resources may be considerably higher than the cost of providing them. Conversely, where an installation has a temporary excess of capacity, lowering the price of services to external users below their average cost (but above their marginal cost) may generate sufficient growth in external usage to provide a net financial benefit to the center.

Having made the point that prices need not rigidly adhere to accounting costs, it must also be stressed that there are potential dangers in trying to influence users through pricing without some clear economic basis for doing so. In particular, manipulation of prices in order to match demand to available capacity is no substitute for long-term efforts to make the appropriate capacity adjustments. For example, an installation that finds itself with a shortage of main memory may deal with this by increasing the rates for memory well above its economic cost or introducing a surcharge for large jobs. While this eliminates the symptoms of the shortage, the underlying problem remains; such price manipulation can only be justified as a stopgap measure while efforts are made to add memory capacity so as to meet the real demand.

It should also be pointed out that once pricing deviates from the firm basis provided by conventional cost accounting principles, it can become a subject of considerable controversy. Pricing that has no demonstrable accounting basis may be considered arbitrary by users and needs to be justified to them. It is all too easy for a computer center manager to use prices primarily to further his own parochial aims, rather than to further the interest of the organization as a whole; for example, a huge price differential between peak-period and off-peak rates may result in a smooth installation work load and high machine utilization, but only at the expense of considerable user inconvenience. This danger—and users' perception of it—makes pricing an even trickier problem. Ultimately, the ability of a computer center manager to safely take an active role in influencing users through pricing will depend entirely on the general level of confidence in that manager, and the extent to which such an active role is regarded as consistent with his responsibilities.

Desirable Characteristics of a Pricing Scheme. It is important that users actively respond to their charges in handling their computing activities; sophisticated pricing will be of little value if charges are simply ignored. These considerations point to several desirable characteristics in the design of a pricing scheme.

First, users must generally accept the pricing scheme as *equitable.* This does not necessarily imply that prices must adhere rigidly to accounting costs, but any deviations from such a cost basis—particularly involving discrimination between users—will probably have to be justifiable to the user community. Apparent inequities that result in a class of users feeling that it is bearing more than its fair share of costs are likely to produce strong reactions and prove a continual source of tensions.

More significantly, the scheme must be *understandable* to users if they are to be able to trace the cause of variations in charges, intelligently seek ways of reducing them, and generally effectively budget for and control their computing activities. As we have already said, pricing schemes are frequently made overly complex and technical in an attempt to measure accurately every aspect of a task's use of system resources; such accuracy may be unnecessary and positively harmful if achieved at the expense of user comprehension. A recent survey of industrial firms revealed that:

> The majority of user/managers interviewed did not understand their data processing charge-out bills anywhere near the level assumed by the designers of charge-out systems. Consequently, the actual control effects of most charge-out systems were a sham. User/manager control actions were assumed to be motivated by deliberation on charge-out bills; in fact, the actions were usually taken for other reasons.[4]

The importance of a concern for user understanding cannot be overemphasized. It involves more than suitable design of the pricing scheme. Educational efforts are needed to explain the scheme and introduce changes. It may also be helpful if computer center staff work with line managers in reviewing their charges and budgeting for future expenditures.

Another important characteristic of a pricing scheme is that it should, as far as possible, yield charges that depend only on factors that are *controllable* by the user. (This is, of course, a principle that applies to any budgetary control system.) Thus, if a user can make his program more efficient or eliminate an unnecessary report from a management information system, his charges should change to reflect his actions—and should do so in a predictable manner. On the other

[4]R. L. Nolan, *Management Accounting and Control of Data Processing* (National Association of Accountants, June 1977).

hand, changes that are outside the user's control, such as variations in the installation loading or configuration changes, should affect the charges for a given processing task as little as possible.[5] Variations in charges over which the user has no control lead to frustration and seriously hinder effective budgetary control.

A particular requirement that arises from the controllability consideration is that the pricing scheme should give *reproducible* results. That is, when a particular job is run on the installation under conditions that vary outside the user's control, the charge for the job should remain reasonably constant. The next section discusses some of the difficulties involved in satisfying this requirement within a multiprogramming environment.

Finally, closely related to controllability, there is a need for *stability* in the charging structure. Price adjustments are occasionally needed to take account of changes in the cost structure (e.g., due to configuration changes) and shifts in the pattern of demand. Moreover, experimentation with pricing can greatly increase the computer center's understanding of its market. Nevertheless, frequent changes in the charging structure weaken users' ability to budget for and control their charges, and frustrates those who base design decisions on a particular charging structure only to find it change to favor a different technical approach a few

[5]Note that this consideration may lead to a basis for pricing that does not strictly reflect the cost of resources used. For example, if a job incurs greater system overheads when the machine is busy, this should not be reflected in increased charges (except, of course, to the extent that this reflects an explicit policy of premium pricing during peak periods).

months later. Therefore, both prices and the underlying basis for calculating charges should be altered as infrequently as possible—particularly in the middle of a budgetary period—and maximum notice should be given when a change is necessary.

Establishing a Price Structure

In any installation there is a large range of resources that could, in theory, be charged for individually. In practice, given the difficulty of accounting for the use of each resource and the need to keep the charging structure simple, organizations typically select a subset of key resources whose usage forms the basis for billing; the rates for these resources are then set to recover not only their direct costs, but also all the other costs associated with the installation. Associated with each resource is one or more utilization measures (some common examples are shown in Figure 4.1); these measures are combined with associated unit prices to define the formula, or "algorithm," through which charges are calculated.[6]

[6]It is common for installations to define usage measures for the various machine resources in terms of a common "work unit" (i.e., so many CPU seconds represent one work unit, so many input-output requests, etc.), and then to establish a price per work unit of resource usage. There is no basic difference in the way charges are calculated under this approach, but it has the advantage that charges can be simply presented in terms of work units, so that users do not have to be concerned with the technical details of individual resource measures. Note, though, that this is of value primarily in an environment where users control only the functional, and not the technical, characteristics of their computing work. Where users develop their own systems—as is normal, for example, in an academic computing

Figure 4.1. *Common resource utilization measures*

Resource category	Measure	Definition
Central system	CPU time	Central processor time used
	I/O time	Total time job occupied input-output channels
	I/O requests	Total number of input-output requests issued by job
	Program size	Job's memory requirement
	Memory time	Integral over time of job's memory requirement
	Productive memory time	As above, but limited to periods during which job had control of CPU
	Swap time	Total time spent swapping pages for job, in a system with paging overheads
Unit record peripherals	Cards read Cards punched Lines printed Plotting time Plotting units	self-explanatory
Data storage	Track days	Integral over time of number of tracks of on-line disc storage occupied by user
	Peak tracks	Maximum number of tracks of on-line storage occupied during the accounting period
	Tape days	Integral over time of number of tape reels reserved by user

environment—they need a breakdown of charges by resource category in order to optimize the efficiency of these systems.

| Terminals and ports | Connect time | Total time user logged onto system from an on-line terminal |
| Operator time | Set-ups | Number of special requests to mount tapes, discs, special printer stationery, etc. |

We describe below how a basic price structure of this sort can be developed, focusing on the considerations involved in selecting the resources to be charged for, designing suitable utilization measures, and setting the prices associated with these measures. We are limited here to a fairly brief discussion of what is a highly complex technical problem, but there is an extensive literature available as a source of further information.[7]

Selecting Resources to Be Charged For. The key consideration in deciding what resources are to be charged for directly is that it is on this subset of resources that users' attention will be focused by the charge-out system. Thus, the resources chosen should reflect the key cost elements in the installation's budget, and those

[7]See, for example: N. R. Nielsen, "Flexible Pricing: An Approach to the Allocation of Computer Resources," *Proceedings AFIPS Fall Joint Computer Conference*, 1968, pp. 521–531; J. T. Hootman, "The Pricing Dilemma," *Datamation*, August 1969, pp. 61–66; C. B. Kreitzberg and J. H. Webb, "An Approach to Job Pricing in Multi-programming Environment," *Proceedings AFIPS Fall Joint Computer Conference, 1972*, pp. 115–122; H. M. Gladney, D. L. Johnson and R. L. Stone, "Computer Installation Accounting," *IBM Systems Journal*, no. 4, 1975, pp. 314–339; M. M. Lehman, "Computer Usage Control," *Computer Journal*, vol. 16, no. 2, (May 1973), pp. 106–110; G. K. Wiorkowski and J. J. Wiorkowski, "A Cost Allocation Model," *Datamation* (August 1973), pp. 60–65.

that are most directly controllable by the user. The main emphasis should be on the most heavily utilized resources, i.e., those that impose the main limitation on installation usage. For example, in some dedicated time-sharing installations, capacity is primarily limited in terms of a maximum number of terminals that can be supported at any one time, irrespective of the type of work each is doing. In such a case charges are best made purely on the basis of terminal connect time, without reference to processor, memory, and I/O channel utilization.

There are difficult tradeoffs in deciding the range of resources to be directly charged for. If too few resources are used as a basis for charging, unacceptable inequities may result. For example, in an installation charging purely on the basis of central processor usage, those users with a primarily computationally oriented work load are likely to feel they are bearing an unreasonably high proportion of the installation costs, in comparison with, say, time-sharing users. More significantly, perhaps, omission of key resources from the pricing scheme may result in distortion of user behavior and lack of control over usage of the resource involved. For example, if input-output operations are not charged for on an installation, programmers may concentrate completely on minimizing factors that are charged for such as central processor time and memory occupancy, while ignoring completely the input-output efficiency of their programs. Peripheral channels may rapidly become a bottleneck under these circumstances.

On the other hand, inclusion of an excessive range of resources in the charging structure, beyond that needed to achieve a reasonable degree of equity and control over resource usage, will simply result in a scheme that is expensive to operate and confusing to the user. A suggested rule of thumb is that a maximum of ten separate charging parameters ought to be used for processing services.

Because hardware used to be the main cost element in computer installations, charging has traditionally been based entirely on machine usage with the cost of services such as application software libraries and user support typically "bundled" into the machine usage charges. However, the cost of these nonhardware-related services has grown to the point where it is as significant as the hardware in many installations' budgets. There are, therefore, now strong arguments for charging directly for these services, to control demand for them, and to avoid subsidy of those who use them by those who need only basic hardware resources. Indeed, as hardware continues to get cheaper in relation to other computing costs, one can envisage a situation where an installation might bundle its hardware resources into the charges for its other services, in the same way that installations have in the past bundled software and support into their hardware resource charges.

Another advantage of unbundling software and support services arises in the common situation where many users have their own minicomputer or use outside services rather than using the central facility. Such users may well still find valuable some of the nonhardware-related services offered by the central facility, such as user support services, programming services, etc., and it will be in the interests of the central systems organization to provide these services. However, where the facility bundles the cost of these services into its processing charges, it has no easy way of providing and charging for such services to nonusers of its hardware resources. Unbundling enables the facility to offer its processing and its support services entirely independently.

Designing Utilization Measures. Associated with the selection of resources to be charged for is the choice of parameters to measure the usage of these resources; for example, use of a machine's input-output channel capacity can be measured in terms of number of I/O requests issued, number of characters transferred, total time over which I/O channels were tied up, etc. Several considerations arise in designing suitable utilization measures.

First, it must be borne in mind that just as the choice of resources charged for affects the direction of users' attention, so does the choice of utilization measures; for example, a user charged for input-output in terms of total characters transferred is unlikely to be concerned with choosing efficient block sizes so as to minimize the number of separate I/O requests required for the transfers. Thus, measures should be chosen that motivate efficiency in the use of available capacity. A particular point here is that where a user is able to prevent others from using a resource even when he is not using it himself, he should pay a penalty for this.[8] Thus, if the memory space reserved for a job is governed by the amount requested by the user on a job control card rather than by the actual program size, then any charge for memory occupancy should be based on the former rather than the latter measure.

The need for understandability, controllability, and reproducibility in the pricing scheme should also be considered in selecting utilization measures. For example, charging for data entry resources on the basis of a count of cards or records punched provides the user with a more meaningful and controllable measure than the administratively more convenient alternative of using total punching hours. A particularly difficult problem in a multiprogramming environment is the identification of measures that accurately reflect resource usage while yielding reproducible results. This difficulty arises because in such an environment, the time taken to run a job and the resources it uses (particularly if system overheads such as page swapping are taken into account) are directly dependent on the installation's overall work load at that time. The problem can be illustrated with reference to the measurement of a job's use of main memory. The obvious measure here would be a function of the job's memory occupancy and its run time. But, in a multiprogramming environment, a job's run time is artificially extended by contention with other concurrent tasks, to an extent dependent on

[8]Hootman (op. cit.) refers to this as the "principle of demurrage."

the installation work load. Thus, charges based on run time would vary with a factor outside the user's control. Instead, it is necessary to define a surrogate measure (such as central processor time) that is reasonably closely related to run time, but is independent of installation work load.

A further factor limiting the choice of utilization measures is the range of data that is relatively easily obtainable from other sources such as a hardware monitor or operators logs. For example, the System Management Facility (SMF) of IBM's Operating System/370 provides a large variety of statistics that are generally used as the main input to charging routines for IBM installations. However, the only statistic available from SMF relative to input-output activity is a count of I/O requests (EXCPs) for each task. Thus, in IBM installations this particular measure is almost always used in charging for input-output resource usage, irrespective of the merits of the theoretical alternatives.

A final point to be made is that the same set of utilization measures need not necessarily be used for all the types of work carried out by an installation. For example, quite different charging formulas might be used for batch and time-sharing work. The charging system described by Lehman[9] embodies four separate schemes for the four main categories of use within the installation.

[9]Lehman, op. cit.

Establishing Prices. Once the basis of charging has been defined, the process of establishing prices is basically that involved in the calculation of standard costs for any service center. The installation's overall revenue requirement (i.e., its costs adjusted by any planned deficit or surplus) is allocated among the resources to be charged for to give a revenue share for each parameter in the charging formula. Dividing each share by the anticipated utilization of that resource yields the associated price per unit. (For example, if $20,000 per month is allocated to the CPU, and the estimated total billable CPU utilization is 500,000 seconds per month, then the rate for CPU usage will be $20,000 divided by 500,000, or 4 cents per CPU second.)

In the allocation process some costs will be clearly attributable to a particular resource, while others (including any general subsidy or profit) will have to be distributed across the various charging elements in some way. In general, the aim will be to ensure that each resource bears its "fair" share of the facility's overall cost recovery target. However, for reasons pointed out in the previous section, the allocation process needs to be carried out flexibly, taking into account not only the general desire that the price of a resource should accurately reflect its cost, but also the overriding consideration that the price structure should induce the desired behavior among users.

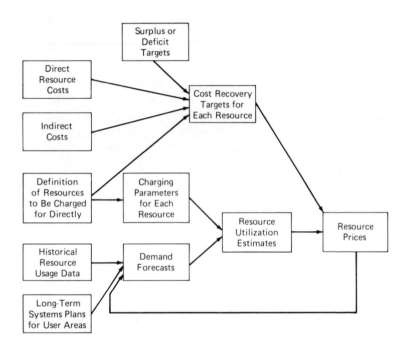

Figure 4.2. Idealized representation of the pricing process

Alternative Pricing Methods

There are other ways of pricing an installation's services that can be used instead of, or in conjunction with, the approach described above. These alternative methods can have considerable advantages in dealing with certain types of resource or service.

Output-Related Pricing. Pricing services in terms of physical resource usage is most appropriate where the installation is primarily supplying raw computing resources with users controlling the way these resources are employed. Where the installation provides information processing services rather than raw resources (as with administrative EDP applications), an alternative is to price these services in terms of the outputs provided rather than the resources used in producing these outputs. For example, a routine sales accounting application might be charged for on the basis of the number of invoice and payment transactions processed with the set price for each type of transaction covering validation, update, and production of standard reports. Similarly, payroll processing might be priced at a standard fee per paycheck with additional charges to cover nonstandard inputs such as special deductions that create additional work. Again, information retrieval services might be priced in terms of a charge per inquiry and/or per item retrieved.[10]

[10]Many practitioners refer to this technique as "transaction-related" pricing. However, this term is often associated with a limited view of the technique in which it is assumed that prices must be set in terms of input

The key advantage of this approach is that users' charges are based on parameters that they can understand and control, rather than on resource-related measures that have no direct meaning in terms of the application involved. To quote a data processing executive within a large insurance company:

> Our users have been budgeting for premiums collected for about 112 years, and they should be reasonably competent at doing that. They shouldn't have to think in terms of the units that the people in the back rooms use to generate the product.[11]

Moreover, with output-related pricing the computer center, which typically controls the development and operation of the application systems, has a financial incentive to ensure that the application work is processed efficiently; when the center charges directly for resources consumed, the user bears the cost of inefficient programs and operational procedures even though he cannot control these factors.

These advantages have understandably led to the widespread adoption of output-related pricing among commercial bureaus offering EDP services. Its use

---

transactions, such as orders processed in an order-entry system. The range of applications in which input transactions alone form a suitable basis for pricing is rather limited; there is no reason why any combination of parameters meaningful in terms of the application should not be used. For example, for an accounts receivable system, charges might be based not only on input transaction volumes (e.g., invoices and payments processed), but also on system outputs (e.g., a charge for each type of report printed), and on data base volumes (e.g., a charge based on the number of active accounts).

[11]Remark by F. Kirshenbaum, quoted in J. C. Emery and H. L. Morgan, "Management and Economics of Data Base Management Systems," in D. A. Jardine ed., *Data Base Management Systems* (New York: American Elsevier/North-Holland, 1974), p. 192.

within internal computer centers is as yet very limited, probably largely because such centers tend to regard charging primarily as a cost allocation mechanism rather than as a control process. However, research has shown that where output-related pricing has been adopted—typically, within organizations with fairly mature data processing activities—it has generally produced a major improvement in the acceptability and effectiveness of charging.[12]

Pricing of services in output-related terms involves estimating the resources that will be used for each unit to be charged for (e.g., per accounting transaction, per data base inquiry, etc.), and then applying standard unit resource prices established for internal use within the center in the manner discussed in the previous section. Clearly, the output-related units used for charging will have to have fairly well defined resource requirements to allow reliable estimation of costs. In an information retrieval application, for example, it will probably be necessary to charge partly in terms of number of inquiries and partly in terms of number of items retrieved, to reflect the effect of both these factors on resource usage. Moreover, if there are different types of inquiry with widely different processing costs, a separate rate may have to be established for each type. Similarly, in a payroll application different prices per paycheck may be used for employees paid on an hourly, weekly, or monthly basis.

As with resource-related pricing, the charging

[12]See Nolan, op. cit.

parameters chosen need to be related to those factors under the user's control that affect the volume of resources used. For example, if punching and processing costs are affected by the accuracy and legibility of coding forms supplied by the user, then it is desirable that charges be based on some measure of this (e.g., number of validation rejections), as well as simple volumes. Similarly, if late submission of data by users causes scheduling difficulties, some standard scale of surcharges may be applied to discourage this practice.

A final point is that there is no reason why output-related pricing should not be used in parallel with resource-related pricing where the latter method is still more appropriate for some users (as with a university installation serving both academic and administrative users). Furthermore, it may often be appropriate to employ a combination of output-related and resource-related prices. In an on-line information retrieval application, for example, a terminal connect charge may be needed in addition to the output-related charges to discourage users from tying up access ports longer than necessary. Similarly, in batch processing applications involving variable amounts of printing, it may be easiest to charge directly for this aspect of resource usage.

Flat-Rate Pricing. In many cases it is possible to offer users the opportunity to contract for resources on a flat-rate, usage-independent basis. For example, access ports to a time-sharing system can be priced on an annual lease basis, as can blocks of disc storage space. Similarly, use of a specialized software package can be charged for through a fixed "usage license" fee. It is even possible to price an entire machine in this way; Dartmouth College currently offers the following alternative in its rate schedule:

> Flat-rate contracts are available on an annual basis to educational institutions; a contract provides dedicated access to a port on the system for 9 or 12 months, up to 100,000 words of storage for files (distributed as the institution desires among its user numbers), and a run-time limit of 8 seconds per job. The run-time limit, which applies each time RUN is typed, can be up to 64 seconds for two users in each flat-rate group. Background use is not included in the flat-rate package but, like extra storage, may be allowed at an extra charge upon application to Kiewit. The charge for a flat-rate contract for 12 months is $600.00 per month, and for 9 months is $660.00 per month.[13]

This form of pricing can provide significant benefits. It reduces the uncertainty in revenue and demand faced by the computer center, as well as the uncertainty in budgeting for computing faced by the user. Moreover, it allows the computer center to reward those users who are able and willing to commit to a given level of resource usage (through flat-rate prices that represent a lower cost per unit than the normal usage-related prices), while still providing other users with the flexibility they require (at a correspondingly higher cost). From the organization's viewpoint, the fact that users' charges are independent of usage means that they are more likely to fully utilize the resource whose cost is typically largely fixed. Note, though, that

[13]Kiewit Computation Center, Dartmouth College: rate schedule in effect July 1, 1976.

this same fact may mean that direct restrictions have to be imposed to limit users' consumption of resources; the Dartmouth example quoted above provides an illustration of this.

Note also that it is possible to combine flat-rate with usage-related pricing in order to gain some degree of stability in computer center revenue while still obtaining the advantages of usage-related pricing in controlling user behavior. For example, charges may be made on a usage-related basis, but with a fixed minimum charge. Or flat-rate charges may be set to cover the fixed costs involved in providing the service and supplemented by usage-related charges intended to recover the variable costs.

Differential Pricing. Differential pricing refers to any situation in which the same resource or service is priced at different rates under different conditions. This technique can be used for a number of purposes; these include:

Indirectly charging for certain resources. For example, higher rates may be applied to those users who require support services than those who only wish to make use of the installation's processing capacity. Or a surcharge on normal rates may be made for jobs employing a particular software package. These differentials provide a means of unbundling these resources from the normal processing charges without going to the lengths of separately accounting for their use.

Discriminating between users, when this is desired. An obvious example is the use of different rates for internal and external users of the center.

Discriminating between different levels of resource usage. An example is a disc storage charge that reduces as a user's file volume increases (e.g., two cents per track per day for the first 1,000 tracks, plus one cent per track per day above this level); this provides a volume discount for large-scale users. Similarly, the opposite technique (i.e., volume surcharges) might be used to actively discourage large-scale use of disc storage—perhaps to encourage such users to move their files off-line.

Distinguishing between different qualities of service in terms of priority, response time, time of day, etc. This technique is discussed more fully below.

Pricing Service Priority

The Priority Problem. Any shared computer facility faces the problem of assigning priorities to the work of competing users. The problem can, of course, be ignored by operating on a simple first-come, first-served basis. However, an explicit priority assignment mechanism can improve the overall value of the installation's service by taking into account differences between users' turnaround needs. For example, if one user badly needs his results in order to continue urgent work while another is relatively indifferent to a delay in obtaining his, it would clearly be in the organization's interest to process the first user's work first, irrespective of who was in the queue earlier.

A related problem occurs with installations that face variations in demand over daily, weekly, or seasonal cycles, or peaks associated with organizational activities such as payroll preparation or end-of-month reporting. These variations result in congestion (with its associated costs in terms of users' time and inconvenience) during peak periods and/or excessive idle capacity (with its associated opportunity costs) at other times. Given these costs it is normally worthwhile to shift work from high-demand to low-demand periods—for example, by deferring work for overnight or weekend processing—even though this inconveniences the users affected. Again, the overall value of the installation's service will be maximized if deferral is applied selectively to those users who would be least inconvenienced.

Direct versus Indirect Control. The discrimination between users involved in both the above areas can be controlled entirely by the computer center. For example, the center can establish set criteria as to which categories of work are to be given high priority, which are to be deferred overnight, etc. However, this approach has the disadvantage that it places on the center the burden of judging between competing users' claims for priority. A generally preferable alternative—particularly in a job-shop environment—is to control the allocation of service priority through the charging mechanism. By offering a range of service qualities, each associated with a different charging rate, users can be left to decide for themselves what service level they feel is worth paying for given their particular needs. Through a suitable pricing scheme, all users can be made better off: users needing fast turnaround or peak-period service can be sure of obtaining it (at a premium price), users not needing this are charged a price lower than they would get under a uniform price structure, while those able to assign work to the lowest priorities or · overnight and weekend periods are charged an even lower price. Decentralization of control in this way provides the advantages that have already been mentioned relative to decentralization in other areas—i.e., replacement of an unwieldy, often inflexible, and highly political direct control process with an impersonal mechanism which influences users through economic incentives while leaving control in their hands.

Pricing Techniques and Considerations. Several methods of pricing service priority are available. They include:

Surcharges for handling "rush" or priority work

In a job-shop environment, multiple batch processing input queues that are given different priorities in scheduling, charging rates rising with priority.

Users specify the priority when submitting a job and pay the appropriate rates.

Reduced rates for evening, overnight, or weekend processing and/or premium rates for peak-period processing

For time-sharing services, varying rates for different times of day or week to encourage users to utilize off-peak periods

In each case, the price differentials between service classes must be sufficiently high to eliminate congestion in the high-priority queues and peak periods so that high-quality service is available at least in these premium classes. More generally, price differentials need to be set so that the range of service levels available satisfies the full spectrum of needs within the user community. Experience has shown that large differentials—up to 60 percent discounts and 250 percent premiums (and thus over a 4 to 1 ratio between highest and lowest rates)—may be necessary to produce an adequate spread. Clearly, the overall rate structure must also satisfy the requirement that the installation's revenue requirements will be met at the anticipated utilization of the various service classes.

A further consideration is the impact of large processing jobs. Tasks that place a heavy load on system resources (e.g., those with large processing, memory, or input-output requirements) have a disproportionately deleterious effect on job turnaround times and total throughput (or response times in the case of time-sharing use). It is therefore worthwhile making specific efforts to shift these particular tasks out of high-priority and peak-period service classes. This can be done through direct restrictions, e.g., "no high priority jobs over 5 minutes' run time," or "all job output over 100 pages will be stored for overnight printing." Alternatively, volume discounts and surcharges in the pricing scheme can be used to achieve the same result in a more flexible manner. For example, Nielsen describes a scheme used at Stanford University to discourage long jobs during the busy daytime hours:

> Rather than charging one of a set of rates for the entire amount of compute time, a step function is used. There is a base rate for daytime computing and a somewhat lower base rate for overnight computing. During the day the base rate is increased by 50% for all time in excess of five minutes and by 100% for all time in excess of ten minutes. During the night the rate is reduced by approximately 7% of the base rate after every thirty minutes of continuous processing by a job. Thus long jobs, which are discouraged during the day, are encouraged at night.[14]

Charging for Systems and Programming Resources

So far our discussion has centered around the problems of charging for processing resources—hardware, common software, and associated support services. We now turn to the considerations involved in charging for resources used in developing and maintaining application

[14]Nielsen, op. cit.

systems where the central facility provides these services.[15]

When to Charge. Explicit charging of system development and enhancement costs forces users to weigh these costs (along with operating costs) against the expected benefits in deciding whether to commission any work. Charging of these costs is, therefore, generally advisable in the interests of ensuring effective use of systems and programming resources for the same reasons that argue for charging for processing resources. However, the effectiveness of charging for development resources is dependent on users having a reliable estimate of implementation costs and the ability to evaluate the anticipated benefits.[16] Where these conditions are not satisfied—as, for example, in an organization new to the use of computers with users unfamiliar with computer applications—it may be preferable to centralize decisions on the deployment of systems and programming resources; in such cases the associated costs are normally best treated as part of the organization's general overhead. Also, where systems and programming resources are only used on a small scale and

[15]The issue of charging for systems development and maintenance naturally does not arise where user organizations handle these functions themselves on a decentralized basis. While a discussion of these organizational questions is beyond the scope of this paper, it should be noted that they will be greatly influenced by the charge-out policies for system development, in the same way that charge-out policies for processing resources influence the extent to which these resources are centralized or decentralized.

[16]Ideally, some form of cost-benefit analysis should be a formal requirement prior to the initiation of any major development project.

constitute only a small proportion of total computing costs, it may not be worthwhile charging for them explicitly; in this case the associated costs can be bundled with the processing charges (as is typically done with user support services).

The trend toward sharing of software within an organization raises some difficult charge-out problems. The cost of developing application software that is expected to be widely used throughout an organization should obviously not be borne solely by the organizational unit that first installs it. In such instances the central systems department should bear the initial cost, which can then be allocated among users either as an overhead item or, preferably, on a usage-related basis (e.g., through a "usage license" fee or through a surcharge on normal processing rates). Naturally, any additional costs incurred in installing or adapting the software for use by another user should be borne directly by that user. As an alternative to central funding, the initial pilot user may in some cases be willing to implement the software on an entrepreneurial basis, bearing all the development costs itself and recovering them through charges levied on subsequent users.

Different considerations apply to the treatment of ongoing maintenance costs for application systems (that is, costs related to correcting errors in the system, adjusting to operating system changes, etc., rather than to implementing enhancements requested by the user). Given that these systems are normally developed by the computer center, there are strong arguments for maintenance costs being borne by the center, since they depend mainly on factors under its control (i.e., the quality of the original programming and testing). In this case maintenance costs are best treated as an overhead within the computer center. Alternatively, a fixed maintenance charge (based, for instance, on a percentage of the initial implementation cost) may be made for each system with the computer center bearing any variance between this charge and actual costs.

Basis for Charging. Development costs are usually charged out in terms of man-days of systems and programming resources used, along with nonpersonnel-related costs such as computer time used for programming and testing. The daily rates for systems and programming staff should be based on expected costs, including overheads such as fringe benefits, office space, etc.; the rates should also allow for a proportion of unbillable time due to lack of work, vacation, sickness, training, etc. Standard rates should be set for each grade of staff (e.g., junior programmer, senior programmer, etc.), rather than using a single average figure for all skill levels or establishing a separate salary-related rate for each individual. (The problem with the latter approach being that project costs then depend on personnel assignment decisions over which neither the user nor the project manager has any control.)

As an alternative to charging on a "time and materials" basis, the computer department may quote a fixed implementation price at the beginning of the project and bear any variance between this and the actual implementation costs. This is likely to encourage efficient implementation by the computer department, and provides the user with a reliable cost estimate on which to base his implementation decision. One difficulty with this approach is that at the beginning of a project the user's requirements, as well as the difficulties of implementation, are often not clear. A fixed-price agreement can thus open the computer department to considerable risk, and may well result in considerable waste of time and effort in attempts at renegotiation and arguments as to what was and was not included in the original quote. One way of reducing these dangers is to begin any implementation project with a "time and materials" pilot study whose objective is to develop the design of the proposed system to a sufficient extent that a firm quote for full implementation can be given with confidence (with the user having the option to abandon the project at that point).[17]

Capitalizing System Development Costs. System development costs can be charged directly against users' operating budgets on the same basis as processing charges; alternatively, they can be charged to users' capital accounts and depreciated over the anticipated life of the system. If system development charges are treated as operating expenses, the impact of these charges on users' operating budgets is likely to distort their decisions on whether, and when, to initiate major

[17]For a discussion of the factors involved in estimating system implementation costs, see C. E. Walston and C. P. Felix, "A Method of Programming Measurement and Estimation," *IBM Systems Journal,* vol. 16, no. 1, 1977.

systems projects; since system development represents an investment of resources made with the expectation of long-term benefits, capitalization will generally be a more appropriate treatment, except for projects that are on such a small scale that capitalization is not worthwhile. The capital budgeting process provides a far more appropriate framework for implementation decisions: not only does it avoid the distortions mentioned above, it also ensures that the formal cost-justification that is normally applied to other forms of capital expenditure is also applied to systems projects.[18]

Special Pricing Problems

Charging for Data Bases.[19] A common organizational data base represents a shared resource with large implementation and operating costs. The way these costs are treated can significantly affect the probability that such a data base is created and the effectiveness with which it is used.

Organizations often treat the cost of implementing a common data base as a current operating expense.

[18]Note, however, that the normal practice with most capital projects of reducing all costs and benefits to a single measure of financial return may not be appropriate in the systems area where a large proportion of benefits are often intangible (see K. E. Knutsen and R. L. Nolan, "Assessing Computer Costs and Benefits," *Journal of Systems Management,* (February 1974), pp. 28–34).

[19]This section is largely based on J. C. Emery and H. L. Morgan, "Management and Economics of Data Base Management Systems," published in D. A. Jardine ed., *Data Base Management Systems* (New York: American Elsevier/North-Holland, 1974), pp. 185–193.

However, as with system development, it is more appropriate to treat these costs as capital expenditures, since they are intended to yield long-term benefits. A manager will be unduly inhibited from undertaking a data base consolidation project if it would produce a large drain on his or her operating budget, particularly in an organization which emphasizes short-term results.

A related problem is the allocation of the implementation cost of a data base within the organization. If, say, a corporate division decides to implement a common data base, then the implementation cost should be borne at that level (i.e., as a divisional overhead). Allocating the costs below this level serves no clear purpose, since it is unlikely to alter actual costs or the original implementation decision. Moreover, charging out implementation costs on top of operating costs on a usage-related basis is likely to result in underutilization of the data base.[20]

The ongoing operating costs associated with the data base also have to be dealt with somehow. The costs of retrieving and processing information for specific applications should, of course, be charged to the users

[20]The principle being applied here is a general one: *charges should be levied at the lowest organizational level at which decisions are made that can significantly influence costs or efficiency.* Processing charges are normally levied against individual users because their decisions on computer usage affect the load on the installation and hence, indirectly, the installation costs. On the other hand, the implementation costs of shared software or data bases are not affected by their volume of usage—in fact, it is in the organization's interests to maximize their usage. Thus, these implementation costs should be borne at the point where the implementation decision was taken, and not by lower-level users.

involved, and can be handled through the normal mechanism for charging for processing. The costs of data collection and storage (both clerical and computer-related) present a more difficult problem. Where the data are widely, and fairly evenly, used throughout the organization, these costs may be treated as an overhead. Otherwise, actual use of the data base (in terms of number of accesses, volume of data transferred, or volume of data stored) can be measured—a sampling method will normally suffice—and costs allocated proportionately.

In many cases users incur significant expense to provide data that are employed elsewhere in the organization. This raises the possibility of a "reverse charging" arrangement through which the data center compensates suppliers of data for the costs of their data collection activities and passes these costs on to the end users of the data. Such an arrangement might increase the supplier's motivation to provide timely and accurate data, and would ensure that end users' charges reflect the full cost of the data they employ. However, to our knowledge, no organization is as yet operating on this basis.[21]

Multiple Processing Facilities. Special considerations arise where an organization operates several processing facilities. In this situation management will wish to ensure that work is distributed among the facilities in

[21]For a further discussion of this idea, see R. L. Nolan, "Restructuring the Data Processing Organization for Data Resource Management," *Proceedings of the IFIP International Conference,* 1977.

a way that takes account of their comparative advantages (for example, a powerful machine may be best suited to large-scale computation, whereas a minicomputer may be more efficient for interactive work), and at the same time produces reasonably balanced machine loading.

If management pursues these objectives by centrally controlling the assignment of work, it will be desirable to price services to users so that their charges are independent of the machine to which their work is assigned. The common practice of setting rates independently for the different facilities so that each recovers its costs will not normally provide this machine independence; instead, the installations' costs and revenues should be pooled. Ideally, a universal set of charging parameters should be chosen with prices for each installation set so that a given unit of "work" costs the same on any machine (so that, for example, a machine with a processor twice as fast as another would be priced at double the rate per CPU second). As an alternative to resource-related pricing, output-related pricing, which is completely machine independent, may be used where appropriate.

If users are left free to choose the installation they will use, the pricing structure needs to be designed to motivate the desired distribution of work. Again, independent pricing of each installation will not necessarily achieve this. For example, a new machine is likely to have lower costs per unit of capacity than older, less technologically advanced installations. If each installation is priced to recover its costs, the new one will be cheaper and will become congested while the other remains underutilized. Clearly, the organization's interests would be better served if, say, the old installations were subsidized to bring their prices down to the level of the newer one.[22]

Competing with Decentralized Resources. A similar problem arises from the existence of alternatives to the computer center, such as local minicomputers and outside services. Again, the computer center's price structure should in general be designed so that if users are left free to choose between the center and the alternatives on the basis of comparative charges, their choices will be consistent with the interests of the organization as a whole.

It would appear at first glance that all that is necessary to achieve this objective is to price the computer center's services in a way that accurately reflects their cost. In practice, however, the problem is more complex. Organizations frequently find that users are financially motivated to move away from the central installation when management feels this is against the general interest. If users have freedom of choice, the result may be an undesirably large flow of work away from the central installation, often leaving that installation with high fixed costs that it cannot recover. Alternatively, central management may impose restrictions on users'

[22]In fact, a reduction in the costs recovered on the old machine is not a subsidy in an economic sense; it is simply a formal recognition that the market value of the old machine has been reduced by subsequent technological advances.

freedom to migrate to other sources of supply, which generally leaves users frustrated, and may well result in failure to exploit cases in which minicomputers or outside suppliers have real advantages.

The causes for the failure of the market mechanism in this area are twofold. The first arises from the fixed costs and economies of scale associated with a large shared computer facility. Due to these factors, the actual incremental cost savings produced when a user moves away from the facility—even assuming that capacity will be adjusted in the long term—are normally considerably lower than the savings seen by the user in the form of eliminated charges. The obvious solution here is to subsidize the computer center so as to bring charges closer to incremental costs, rather than average resource costs. However, this decision obviously must take account of wider considerations than those involved here.[23]

Apart from this, though, the form of the installation's charging structure can have a major impact. The services provided by a typical large-scale computer center cover a wide range of user needs, and normally include extensive support services such as user consultants and documentation. Moreover, even though the center's costs are typically fairly fixed, it normally requires no expenditure commitment from users, but provides services essentially on demand and accepts

[23]This possibility is often rejected out-of-hand by those who feel that a computer facility must recover its costs. In our view there is nothing magical about full cost recovery: the issue is whether a subsidy will produce more or less desirable results.

the resulting fluctuations in usage from day to day and year to year. For some users, this generality and flexibility is a necessity; for others—those whose needs are primarily for raw computer power and who are willing and able to make long-term usage commitments—it is not. Computer charging schemes that fail to differentiate between these types of user force the latter to pay for the cost of this generality and flexibility even though they do not need it.

This effect can be a major cause of large discrepancies between the cost savings seen by a user in moving away from the central facility, and those seen at the facility itself. A typical example is that of the university physics department, which needs large quantities of computational power but little support in the form of software packages, documentation, or user services. Under a pricing scheme in which the latter are charged for implicitly as part of the processing rates, such a user may well find it cheaper to set up its own specialized installation, even though the computational resources required can be provided more cheaply (in terms of actual costs to the organization) by the central facility.

The implication is that, as far as possible, the generality and flexibility provided by a large shared facility should be unbundled (i.e., charged for separately) within the center's pricing scheme, so that only those users that need it pay for it. Two techniques in particular are important here. First, major resources such as software libraries and user support services should be charged for directly rather than being bundled in with processing rates: the greater the unbundling of prices, the more each user's charges will reflect only those resources used for his particular application. Second, large-scale users should be offered long-term, flat-rate, or minimum-commitment contracts at discounted rates that exclude the extra costs of handling small-scale users and those with variable usage. This allows the center to compete with dedicated minicomputer installations on equal terms.

5 / INFORMATION AND CONTROL PROVISIONS

Implementation of charging involves developing computer accounting routines and associated administrative procedures. Discussed below are some of the provisions needed within these routines and procedures to support decision making and control by those involved in the charge-out system. They are:

computer center management

line managers in user areas who have responsibility for computing budgets

end users of computer services

In general, the job-shop environment typical of academic or engineering and research computing normally requires somewhat different administrative and control provisions than are needed in an environment oriented to routine administrative data processing (where the budget administrator is effectively the end user). However, we have tried to make our discussion relevant to both.

Computer Center Management

The measurement of resource usage involved in charging also provides information on the overall installation work load and utilization. Such information can be used in fine tuning the installation's software and hardware configuration, in balancing work load through pricing and other control mechanisms, and in forecasting future usage and revenues. Specific reports that should be available to computer center management include:

> Utilization reports for the various system resources, showing overall utilization for each resource and breakdowns by class of work (e.g. batch, time-sharing, etc.)

> Analyses of installation work load by time of day, type of work, priority, and user category

Breakdowns should be provided in terms of both physical and monetary units. Analyses of variances between actual and budgeted figures should also be available to management.

A further consideration where charges form the basis for cash transactions is the need for provision to audit the charge-out system.

Budget Administrators

Individuals responsible for computing budgets in user subunits need a means of monitoring and controlling the activities within their area of responsibility. This may include not only those with formal budgetary responsibility, but also subordinates such as a project leader, or a faculty member controlling an allocation for instructional use within a class.

Budget administrators should be able to establish separate accounts to cover different users and/or activities under their control. They should be provided with regular reports showing expenditure under these accounts with comparisons against budget. Detailed breakdowns of expenditures should be available that enable managers to trace causes for variances from budget and to seek ways of reducing charges. In an administrative data processing environment such breakdowns should separate costs for each application area and for the various functions and/or outputs within each application; transaction volume figures should also be provided to permit separation of variances due to volume variations and other causes. Where administrators are responsible for a group of users that have direct access to computing resources, they should be able to get breakdowns that show how users are spending their allocations—e.g., by type of processing, by source of supply, or by priority level. Ideally, these facilities would be provided through a flexible report generator that could be used to aggregate the detailed charges as required.

In a job-shop environment, budget administrators also need to be able to control resource consumption by users for whom they are responsible. Control provisions might include, for example:

The ability to limit total expenditure

Where charges vary with priority requested or time of day, the ability to set a maximum priority level and/or limit job submissions to off-peak periods

A means of limiting resource usage through restrictions on program size and run time, disc storage quotas, etc.

A means of limiting the type of computing performed (e.g., batch only, or running of "canned" programs only)

The ability to selectively restrict users to a specific source of supply (e.g., the main computer center only)

Ideally, it should be possible to set these control parameters for each account independently. This enables the budget administrator to tailor the restrictions to each user or group of users. Moreover, where a given user has access to two or more accounts established for different purposes, it should be possible, through restrictions on the accounts, to limit usage on each account to the purposes intended.

End Users

In a job-shop environment, individual users themselves also need to be able to keep track of their own expenditures. Thus, the system should inform the user of the charges for each job or time-sharing session. This information should show how the charge is arrived at as well as the total figure, so that the user can explain changes in his charges, experiment with the effects of alternative technical strategies, etc. The system should also provide the user with an indication of the cumulative charges and remaining allocation in his or her account; this information may be provided along with the job charges or on request.

6 / CONCLUSION

We conclude by returning to our statement at the beginning of this book: to be fully effective, a charge-out system needs to be tailored to the objectives it is to serve and the circumstances within which it will operate. In our experience, charge-out systems are often less valuable than they might be because management has introduced charging as a "good idea," without ever clearly defining precisely what it wishes to achieve thereby. Charging is all too often regarded as a straightforward accounting mechanism, rather than a control tool that can, and should, be tailored to management's needs.

As we have tried to show, there is a large range of options, both in defining the framework within which charging operates and in designing the pricing scheme itself. Managers should consider whether the particular charge-out system employed within their organization is best suited to its current pattern of computing activities and to their own objectives in relation to controlling these activities. For example:

If a "funny-money" allocation system is in use, is it still appropriate? Has it become a focus for political tensions? Does demand for computing seem insatiable with no indication as to where the growth in computer expenditure should stop? Is all computing still done at the central facility without examination of alternative sources such as minicomputers for some activities? If so, a switch to "real money" charging might greatly ease these problems.

Is the computer center underutilized or overloaded? With "funny-money" budgeting, this may indicate that the total allocation of "computer dollars" is too small or too large. With decentralized budgeting, it may be that too rigid an insistence on short-term cost recovery is preventing the computer center from adjusting prices or capacity to match demand and supply.

Do users ignore charges, fail to look for ways to reduce them? In a centralized budgeting environment, it may be that users' computing budgets are so generous that they have no need to control their usage or charges. Alternatively, the pricing scheme may be too complex; a simpler, less accurate basis for charging may be preferable. Perhaps the charging system does not provide users with the information needed to enable them to analyze charges effectively. Or perhaps more effort is needed to educate users in how to interpret charging data.

Would transaction-based pricing give better results?

Are users able to reduce their processing costs by moving their work from the central computer facility even when this is against the organization's interest? Is this causing dissatisfaction in the case of users who are not permitted to move, and/or loss to the organization in the case of those who are? Would greater unbundling help to bring these users' charges closer to the true costs of their processing? Or more flexibility in pricing (e.g., long-term bulk supply contracts priced at marginal cost for those users large enough to obtain their own machines)? Or should a general policy of subsidizing the center be adopted, abandoning the principle of full cost recovery?

Are there usage categories whose exclusion from charging would be justified by savings in overhead and red tape (e.g., students, who may represent, say, fifty percent of total users and sixty percent of jobs processed, but only ten percent of resource utilization)?

Would competing pressures on the computer center be reduced and ability to respond to urgent processing requirements be improved through introduction of time-of-day and/or priority-related price differentials?

Does the computer facility fully exploit imaginative pricing and contracting arrangements such as output-related pricing, long-term bulk contracts, and royalty charges for software use?

Readers will no doubt be able to identify similar problem areas associated with computing within their organization. We are confident that a review of an organization's charge-out system along the lines indicated above, seeking ways to improve its contribution to the control of computing activities, would prove well worthwhile. The potential value of an effective charge-out system is such that it deserves careful attention from senior management, as well as computer center management and users.

FURTHER READING

"Charging for Computer Services." *EDP Analyzer,* July 1974, Canning Publications, Inc.

Cushing, B. E. "Pricing Internal Computer Services: The Basic Issues." *Management Accounting,* April 1976.

Dearden, J. and R. L. Nolan. "How to Control the Computer Resource." *Harvard Business Review,* November–December 1973, pp. 68–78.

"Effects of Charge-back Policies, The." *EDP Analyzer,* Nov. 1973, Canning Publications, Inc.

Emery, J. C. "Problems and Promises of Regional Computer Sharing," in M. Greenberger et al. eds. *Networks for Research and Education.* Cambridge: M.I.T. Press, 1974, pp. 189–198.

Emery, J. C. and H. L. Morgan. "Management and Economics of Data Base Management Systems," in J. A. Jardine ed. *Data Base Management Systems.* New York: American Elsevier/North-Holland Publishing Co., 1974.

Gill, S. and P. A. Samet. "Charging for Computer Time in Universities." *Computer Bulletin,* vol. 13, no. 1, (January 1969), pp. 14–16.

Gladney, H. M., D. L. Johnson and R. L. Stone. "Computer Installation Accounting." *IBM Systems Journal,* no. 4, 1975, pp. 314–339.

Goldstein, D., M. C. Jensen and D. Smith. *Report of the President's Committee on Computing Problems and Opportunities,* University of Rochester, 1973.

Grampp, F. T. "A Computer Center Accounting System." *Proceedings AFIPS Fall Joint Computer Conference,* 1971, pp. 105–114.

Grillos, John M. "Pricing EDP Resources." *Computer Decisions.* November 1974, pp. 16–17.

Grindley, Kit. "Internal Charging for Computer Services." *Accountancy* (Great Britain: March 1973), pp. 32–35.

Grobstein, D. L. and R. P. Uhlig. "A Wholesale Retail Concept for Computer Network Management." *Proceedings AFIPS Fall Joint Computer Conference 1972,* pp. 889–898.

Hootman, J. T. "The Pricing Dilemma." *Datamation,* August 1969, pp. 61–66.

Kanter, H., A. Moore and N. Singer. "The Allocation of Computer Time by University Computer Centers." *Journal of Business,* vol. 41, no. 3, (July 1968), pp. 375–384.

Kreitzberg, C. B. and J. H. Webb. "An Approach to Job Pricing in a Multi-programming Environment." *Proceedings AFIPS Fall Joint Computer Conference, 1972,* pp. 115–122.

Lehman, M. M. "Computer Usage Control." *Computer Journal,* vol. 16, no. 2, (May 1973), pp. 106–110.

Li, D. H. *Accounting for Costs of EDP Service Centers.* Cost Accounting Standards Board, 441 G. St., Washington, D. C., 20548, 1975.

McFarlan, F. W., R. L. Nolan and D. P. Norton. *Information Systems Administration.* New York: Holt, Rinehart & Winston, Inc., 1973, Chapter 11.

Management Guidelines for Cost Accounting and Cost Control for ADP Activities and Systems. Report of Recommendations of the Task Group on Principles, Standards and Guidelines for Management Control of ADP Activities and Systems, U. S. General Accounting Office, September 1975.

Marchand, M. "Priority Pricing with Application to Time-Shared Computers." *AFIPS Fall Joint Comp. Conf. 1968.*

Marchand, M. "Priority Pricing," *Management Science,* vol. 20, no. 7, (March 1974), pp. 1131–1140.

Nielsen, N. R. "Flexible Pricing: an Approach to the Allocation of Computer Resources," *Proceedings AFIPS Fall Joint Computer Conference, 1968,* pp. 521–531.

———. "The Allocation of Computer Resources—Is Pricing the Answer?" *Communications of the ACM,* vol. 13, no. 8, (August 1970), pp. 467–474.

———. "Using Your Computing Resources to Best Advantage." *Journal of Contemporary Business,* Spring 1972, pp. 35–50.

Nolan, R. L. "Preliminary Ideas on Research Design to Investigate Internal Pricing of Computer Resources for Management Control." *Proceedings* of the Wharton Conference on Research on Computers in Organizations, published as *Data Base,* vol. 5, nos. 2, 3 & 4 (Winter 1973).

_____. "Panel Session: Charge-out Systems for Management Acceptance and Control of the Computer Resource." *Proceedings AFIPS National Computer Conference, 1974,* pp. 1013–1016.

_____. "Effects of Chargeout on User/Manager Attitudes." *Communications of the ACM,* vol. 20, no. 3 (March 1977), pp. 177–185.

_____. *Management Accounting and Control of Data Processing.* National Association of Accountants, June 1977.

Popadic, R. P. "Design of Chargeout Control Systems for Computer Services," in W. McFarlan and R. L. Nolan eds. *The Information Systems Handbook.* Homewood, Ill.: Dow Jones-Irwin, 1975.

Reichardt, Karl E. "Capitalizing Costs of Information Systems." *Management Accounting,* April 1974, pp. 39–43.

Rettus, R. C. and R. A. Smith. "Accounting Control of Data Processing." *IBM Systems Journal,* vol. 11, no. 1, (1972), pp. 74–92.

Schaller, C. "Survey of Computer Cost Allocation Techniques." *Journal of Accountancy,* June 1974, pp. 42–46.

Selwyn, L. L. "Computer Resource Accounting in a Time-shared Environment." *Proceedings AFIPS Fall Joint Computer Conference, 1970,* pp. 119–130.

_____. "Computer Resource Accounting and Pricing." *Proceedings 2nd Annual SIGCOSIM Symposium, Oct. 1971,* pp. 14–24.

Sharpe, W. F. *The Economics of Computers.* New York: Columbia University Press, 1969, Chapter 11.

Singer, N., H. Kanter and A. Moore. "Prices and the Allocation of Computer Time." *Proceedings AFIPS Fall Joint Computer Conference, 1968.*

Smidt, S. "Flexible Pricing of Computer Services." *Management Science,* vol. 14, no. 10, (June 1968), pp. B–581–600.

_____. "The Use of Hard and Soft Money Budgets and Prices to Limit Demand for a Centralized Computer Facility." *Proceedings AFIPS Fall Joint Computer Conference, 1968,* pp. 499–509.

Statland, N. et al. "Guidelines for Cost Accounting Practices for Data Processing." *Data Base,* vol. 8, no. 3, Winter 1977 supplement.

Stefferud, E. Untitled paper on wholesale-retail charging schemes, in *Proceedings* SIGMETRICS Technical Meeting on Pricing Computer Services, No. 20–21, 1975, published in *Performance Evaluation Review,* vol. 5C, no. 1, March 1976, pp. 31–70.

Turney, P. B. B. "Transfer Pricing Management Information Systems," *MIS Quarterly,* vol. 1, no. 1 (March 1977), pp. 27–35.

Wiorkowski, G. K. and J. J. Wiorkowski. "A Cost Allocation Model." *Datamation,* August 1973, pp. 60–65.

INDEX